KE...

KEEP IT NAKED™

*A Naked Girlz™ Guide to
Live Life Authentically*

Printed in the United States of America

First Printing, 2016

ISBN 978-0-9979860-1-3

Shemeka Michelle Enterprises LLC
Durham, North Carolina 27703

www.ShemekaMichelle.com

Cover design by Family First! Designs
Front cover photograph by C. Elaine Harris
Front cover photograph edited by Mike C.O.X.
Author photograph by Lacy Smith

DEDICATIONS

◆◇◆

This book is dedicated to my favorite "girlz." The five of you have been the main reasons I have persevered in the midst of despair. I've always wanted to make each and every one of you proud. This book is just one of my many accomplishments. Being a daughter, granddaughter and mom you can be proud of, is by far my greatest accomplishment of all! I love you.

◆◇◆

Mom, you have been the most selfless woman I know. Often times I'm amazed at your ability to love me the way you do. You've never treated me like someone created with a stranger in a moment of pain. For that, I thank and appreciate you. You have held my hand from the very beginning. Take a bow. I couldn't have done this without you.

Grandma, you are the lady in my life who has aged so gracefully. You have done so much for me. I could never repay you but I want to try. If you never take the time to read this book, I will be honored to have it sit amongst your other books as a testament that I did exactly what I told you I would.

My beautiful daughters, when you have your own children, you'll understand all of the "crazy" that makes me your "mama bear." Kaylah, my first born, you make my heart smile. In many ways, we grew up together. Super model, work! Kylah Bug, you are my sunshine, my only sunshine. You brighten my world! Kelyse, you're the queen to be. Keep preparing to take the throne! All of you inspire me to take a licking and keep on ticking. I'm honored to be your mommy.

TABLE OF CONTENTS

INTRODUCTION

◆◇◆

No, I do not want to host a Mary Kay party for you or host a heap of dog shit pyramid scheme. I, also, don't want to spend countless hours doing something I hate in order to make you rich. Honestly, I don't care how much money I can make. If I'm going to be miserable in the process, what's the point? If you believe we only have one life to live, why in the hell would any of us spend most of our adult lives working paycheck to paycheck just to make a bullshit living that still doesn't allow us to live? That sounds completely ridiculous, yet most of us do exactly that day after day. Not only have we done that day after day, we teach our kids to do exactly the same thing. If you happen to have children that don't want to live the same pathetic life day in and day out, you discourage them from discovering and living their purpose because you haven't lived yours. You were scared to take risks. Now, you stare at your wrinkled old ass every morning in the mirror wishing you had done something with your life. Now that your titties are sagging, you wish you would have modeled in your youth. Even though everyone told you that you needed to be a model, you weren't sure if you were pretty enough, so you never took the chance. You wanted to be a public speaker, but now that you're missing teeth on the side of your mouth, you don't have the courage. Although you always spread wisdom in your youth, you got hit with the *one day* syndrome. "One day, I'll follow my dreams. One day, I'll live the life I really want to live. One day, I'll spread knowledge. One day, I'll pursue public speaking," you told yourself. Now you don't like to talk to people because instead of thirty-two teeth in your mouth, you only have fifteen. You could visit a dentist to solve that problem, but you're so used to living a boring life, you have just come to the conclusion that you will never do what you were put on earth to do. You didn't do what you could've done yesterday, so you sit around and shit on everyone else's tomorrow. In your mind, success only happens to special people and let's face it, you don't think you're that special person. In fact, you don't even understand the meaning of real success. To you there is no correlation between success and real happiness because you are a miserable sack of shit. You hate your life but you are too afraid to change it. You have the balls of an unborn male child; they are still up in your guts! Does thinking about your life make you feel butterflies? You wouldn't know your purpose if it rose up and slapped you in the face because you have become content with living an average life of nothingness. Sure there are things that you do well. Of course there are things that you love. However, the fear of failure has caused you to put your dreams and desires on ice. Now you are scared to allow those dreams to thaw. You are unable to pursue your dreams because you just don't have the guts.

This sounds like a bunch of cruel and heartless rhetoric but it's actually me living my purpose. Today I see my strength. I am not only an outspoken individual, but I am also in tune with the universe. I have the ability to cut ties, stand up for myself, speak truth and walk away from anything or anyone that disturbs my peace. I don't waddle long in bullshit. I don't like when people are inauthentic, and I have no problem addressing what many ignore. While some claim to be offended with my direct approach, there are many that have sought me out for just that reason. To these people I say, "Thank you for recognizing in me what took me many years to recognize in myself. You are greatly appreciated and this book is for you. Smooches!"

Chapter 1

◆◇◆

PURPOSE

"We all have a role to fill. Even the seat filler's name rolls in the credits."

"You speak the very oracles of God!" she said to me. Those words were straight bullshit that the pastor was saying to make me think more highly of myself than I should. It's also feel good talk that's often used in churches to increase tithes and offerings. You know, most people give more money when they get a favorable *word from the*

Lord. Nothing could be more favorable than believing I had a direct line to God the Father. The Omniscient One was telling me things for his people that they didn't already know. Although I knew it was a crock of crap, I fell out, slain in the spirit, like a lot of church goers that want to be seen as super holy. However, what she meant was that I'm the person who's going to tell you the truth whether you like it or not. I also don't give a rat's ass what you think about me afterwards. This is one of the traits that most people love about me until they realize they can't control what I say. One of my closest friends told me that I've always been good at talking shit to people. Now, I am doing it for a living. Even when I look back at comments left on the back of pictures or written to me in my yearbook, according to others, I have always had a way with words. They wrote messages to me like "To the girl with the big mouth" or "To the girl that won't shut up." Some even said, "That mouth will take you far."

Author and spiritual teacher, Gary Zukav, states in his book, *The Seat of the Soul*, "When the personality comes fully to serve the energy of the soul, that is authentic power." That statement sounds simple enough but most people still can't figure out their purpose. In my opinion, they can't find their purpose because they don't know their real personality. They don't know their real personality because they are too busy acting and flaunting a fake one. One of my former roommates would often give me the look after I made a statement. I would always look at her and say, "What?" completely clueless that I had said something that may have been offensive. I was simply being Shemeka. I had no idea at the time that just being who I was, was something unusual. I didn't realize then that I would mature and see that most people are on some *straight bullshit.* I don't see how some people look at themselves in the mirror day after day knowing they are looking at a phony. We've all met these people. They are the ones who talk three octaves higher than they normally do when they are around certain people, like someone just shoved a stick in their ass. They have that fake annoying laugh that's neither cute nor real when in certain social circles. Often, they won't even laugh in certain circles because they are too afraid of what others may think if they find a certain joke amusing. These types of people get on my damn nerves.

17

The people that aren't comfortable being themselves are the same ones that aren't comfortable with you being you. They feel obligated to morph into someone else and they expect you to do the same. If they know you are the type of person that is the same all the time, they will eventually stop being around you because it becomes too risky. They will be afraid that someone may see who they really are just by hanging around you. If you are like me, honest with no filter, they'll be afraid that you'll somehow expose them. I've had a lot of so called friends like this. Most of those fake friendships were formed during the years I was heavily involved in the church. As long as I was wearing skirts to my ankles and crediting every positive thing that happened in my life to Jesus, I was a safe person to have as a friend. They knew they could greet me with "Praise the Lord" and I would return their salutation with the same "Praise the Lord." The typical "How are you?" would then be followed by a "Blessed and highly favored." However, once they became unsure of my response because they were being met with a normal "Hello" or a "Shiddd just chillin'" they stopped asking. As long as I was pretending to be the person that made them comfortable, we were the best of

18

friends. However, when I stopped pretending, I was *of the devil* and they had to sever ties with me to keep the devil at bay.

How do you not tire of living a fake life? In my opinion, being fake takes way too much energy and effort to keep up with the lies of being someone you are not. I also think people who can't be themselves don't like who they are in reality. If you can't be who you really are, how can you find your true purpose? People who want to be in the limelight are a dime a dozen. I'm sure we all know people right now who think they have the ability to empower others when they are actually defeated in their own lives. How can you guide people to a better way to live when you don't know yourself? I would much rather be shown how to get to a particular place by someone who has actually been there. You can't give accurate directions if you are lost yourself. I knew that as long as I was in a relationship where I was being mistreated or being called a bitch, I could never show another woman the way out of a bad relationship. As long as I was living a bound and restricted life, I could never tell someone else how to be free. As long as I was living a lie and wearing a mask, I could never tell someone else how to live *naked*. That is like a fat person telling someone else how to get skinny. Unless this fat person tells the truth about his or her bad eating habits and lack of exercise and says, "Don't do what I'm doing," the advice would be a waste of folk's time. Maybe I used that analogy because I am completely annoyed with the fat person that never seems to lose weight but is always giving out diet advice. I also get annoyed with the single person that always has dating advice but shit never seems to work out for him or her. This person can't keep a relationship and never seems happy, but has this keen insight, shared as wisdom and daily quotes, into the world of healthy relationship bliss. However, I digress.

The only true way to realize your purpose is to get to know and love who you really are. What do you like to do? What would you do if there were no checks involved? What brings you total peace even in the midst of chaos? I know that my purpose is to guide people into an authentic place in their lives. I'm here to live transparent, exposing my deepest feelings, not only to free myself, but to facilitate the freedom of others. Everything I do is tied to this purpose. When I blog, I focus on this purpose. When I speak to groups, I focus on this purpose. When I talk to people one on one, I focus on this purpose. When I sat down to write this book, I focused on this purpose - to free myself and to facilitate your freedom. I have several streams of income, but they are all things I love to do because they are within my purpose. If I hadn't decided to take off the masks I was wearing, I would never have been comfortable enough to be myself and to love myself. I would still be crying at night and aging quickly, stressed out over the fact that I seemed to be continually going around the same tree of misfortune.

Over the years, many people have approached me for 'no nonsense' advice. I've always been the type to say exactly what I am thinking without added filters. I've never had the time to sugarcoat anything. If you are great, I have no problem expressing that I think you're the best thing since sliced bread. However, don't expect me to hold my tongue to spare a few hurt feelings if that bread is molded, is dry, or I think you're just full of shit! I believe that the truth will make you free. Family, friends, co-workers, and people I've met online through my blog and social media, acknowledge that I have something to say that needs to be heard. And I'm not afraid to say it. These people saw something in me that I didn't realize was actually an asset. Without knowing it, I was living the art of persuasion. I had the uncanny ability to say what other people were only brave enough to think. Then, even if they were brave enough to think it, it was only for a split second. I, on the other hand, was never really afraid of speaking my thoughts. I was never concerned about my thoughts *sending me to hell.* Before I understood how powerful thoughts were, I would even tell people off in my head using every obscene word imaginable even if I never uttered a sound. However, I've always talked too much and was never able to hide those thoughts for too long. I knew that I possessed many great attributes like most people, but it wasn't until recently that I realized the value of some of my beliefs. It wasn't until recently that I began to value my ability to be myself.

In times past, I have received calls at ridiculous times like three in the morning from women who were dealing with the cares of this world. Most of the time, they were just being silly women. They would seek me out in the middle of the night because they believed I possessed the words of wisdom to set them free. What's extremely funny about this is I was psychologically clueless. I was just being me, saying what sounded like common sense. Although my initial reaction would be "What in *de* hell?" as I looked at the time, I loved being there for people. I never really put much thought into it. I would just always listen to them intently while I listened to my inner voice and then just spoke those words. Once they felt encouraged or strengthened, I would roll over and take my ass back to sleep.

So just why did some people seek me out for advice, men and women, young and old? I can only guess that there was a small, special group of people that saw long before I did, that I was walking the talk. No matter what I believed at the time, I believed it no matter what anyone else said. I believed it until I didn't believe it anymore. If I consider you a friend, I ride with you until the wheels fall off the ride. Let me be clear though, once those wheels are gone, I am not helping your ass get down the street. If you are an unmistakable foe, there is no guessing where I stand. I am that person who doesn't go to great lengths to try and hide my feelings. Sometimes you may not be able to see the emotion that's normally displayed with those feelings but my actions are always in line. If I don't rock with you, trust me, you'll know it!

Chapter 1 Naked Nuggets:

1. KNOW WHO YOU ARE

The only way for you to find your purpose is to know thyself. I went to college and majored in Biology. Although I loved dissecting worms, that really wasn't the major for me. If I had taken time early in my life to get to know myself, I probably would have realized that Communications or even Psychology may have been a better fit.

2. BE YOURSELF

In a world of copy cats it's easy to try to imitate someone else who you deem successful. However, that doesn't normally work out well. Most people can smell a rat a mile away and you'll eventually be exposed for being disingenuous. Not only that, when you are yourself, you don't have to keep up with the lies of a fake character that you've created.

3. BE HONEST

Most people are familiar with the term "fake it until you make it." However, more often than not, honesty is actually the best policy. After all, would you want to be on an operating table awaiting heart surgery from someone in a white lab coat who was faking it? Absolutely not! Instead of presenting yourself as someone you aren't, work on yourself so that you can present to the world your best you!

Chapter 2

◆◇◆

WHO IS SHEMEKA MICHELLE?

"What makes me qualified to give advice? My fucking life!"

For many women, my body should've exploded as I was being sucked through a vacuum tube into nonexistence. It sounds graphic, but that's what happens during an abortion. I can't even say I would have blamed my mom if she had decided to get an abortion. Considering she was raped at the tender age of fourteen by a complete stranger, I don't think anyone else would have balked at the decision either. I cannot even begin to imagine what it must have felt like to have your faith, innocence, joy, trust and security shattered in one moment. I also cannot imagine what it must have been like to have your first encounter with sex take place in a wooded area filled with dirt and insects. Although it is probably a memory she would rather keep buried, she would always recount the events of her rape for me anytime I had questions.

It was a warm spring day, and she didn't expect this day to be any different from the day before. She was headed through a path which was her normal route to a nearby school that was holding tryouts for cheerleading. Tragically, this man must have made note of her routine and waited for her to enter the path alone as usual. Walking towards her, just as she passed him, he turned and grabbed her from behind, holding a knife to her neck. I've never asked about details beyond that point. However, I imagine tears rolling down her face through clinched eyes. Sometimes, I even wonder if she left her body (so to speak) traveling to another place in time where she was safe and not being violated. When her eyes did open, she looked up at a sky that was now overshadowed with evil. Did she hang around the path afterward trying to brush free from debris and picking leaves from her hair? This moment forever changed her life. Although I'm no psychologist, I truly believe there are remnants (other than myself) that linger from that horrific act. I know for a fact that you can't grab my mom from behind, not even jokingly. She doesn't like that! Our family even laughs about the fact that she always has to be in control of every situation. I believe that's a natural behavior for someone who once was taken control of in such a defiling way.

I can't imagine the uproar that would've taken place if my mom had said anything to her family. She had three brothers at the time and I believe the older two would have tried to kill him. Her mom on the other hand, may have been a different story. Don't get me wrong, my grandma is a fabulous lady that I love to no end. After all, she stood in the place of my mom for two years until my mom graduated from high school. Also, because we lived with her until I graduated from high school, she played an instrumental role in my life. I say it may have been another story because my grandma has always been kind of stoic. In thirty-nine years, I don't think I've ever seen her cry. I've seen her be extremely angry and sit quietly when I assume she's sad or depressed, but she has never shown any depth

29

of emotion. I've never witnessed her laugh uncontrollably or even just let loose to her favorite song. She's always supported all of my accomplishments, but I never really knew what she was thinking at any given time. She took great care of all of us, but I certainly didn't learn affection from her.

However, all of these thoughts of what might have happened if my mom had told someone are just mere speculation because my mom, who please be reminded was only fourteen, never told a soul. At the time of the rape, she was still in junior high, but shortly afterwards she was accepted at the prestigious Stuart Hall High School for girls. I remember visiting the school with her as an adult when she went for a reunion. I didn't get the "Facts of Life" feeling I was expecting. It actually seemed like we were invisible to most. It was a predominately white school at the time of her attendance, and it seemed as if not many were excited to see our black faces. I smiled for those that seemed to care but I was really ready to go to the hotel and take a swim in the pool.

Growing up, my mom had dreams of becoming a doctor. After the rape, when it was time for school to begin in the fall, she went to Stuart Hall as planned which was located in Staunton, Virginia. I still have a hard time believing or accepting the fact that my grandma didn't notice that something was different with her daughter. Surely, mentally and emotionally something had changed. However it seems as if back in those days the consensus was to just ignore things with the hope that they would go away. The family didn't find out my mom was pregnant until seven months later. That means that even during Thanksgiving break no one noticed that she had a bun in the oven. Remember this was 1974. My mom was a flesh covered stick figure. She wasn't the size of today's hormone fed beef eating teens. She lacked the curves and extra pounds that would've served in hiding the bulge in this day and time. On top of that, she was extremely sick for most of her pregnancy. Our primary source of nourishment was honey buns and cherry soda. Maybe I'm just nosey (or inquisitive as I prefer to be called), but I think I would've noticed someone hocking up the Thanksgiving turkey and stuffing. The festivities must have been very festive because not one person noticed. Perhaps psychological denial played a part in her physical appearance as well. My mom, with a delivery date in February, was sent to Florence Crittenton in Charlotte, North Carolina, after Christmas break. This was a home for unwed mothers. I experienced visiting this place as well. As I drove onto the property there was a bold "Safe House" sign. I stopped at the gate with the hope that I would be allowed to enter. I wondered if I sounded completely ridiculous to the person on the other end trying to discreetly explain the reason for my visit. Thankfully, she lifted the gate so I could enter.

It was a midsize brick building located across from the hospital where I was born. The receptionist who had let me through was a very pleasant older black lady who really seemed intrigued by my reason for being there. It was chilly and quiet enough for me to hear my own thoughts. It was October but I could hear the sounds of a bird chirping on the patio. The quietness was somewhat unnerving as I can't imagine being fourteen years old, alone in a strange place awaiting the arrival of a strange face due to being impregnated by a stranger. When I was fourteen years old, I was surrounded by friends and a false sense of immortality.

I sat there however and wanted to cry at the thought of my mom being in this place. She must have been so confused. The God that she had learned about in church had allowed her path to lead her here, emotionally detached from the life growing inside of her and clueless about what was ahead. I wanted to cry, but I didn't want to look like a psychopath. I sat and waited for what seemed like forever for a representative to show me the place. The representative seemed happy to see me and introduced me to other employees as a "Florence Crittenton" baby. She explained that the actual building where my mom had lived was torn down a few years after she left. When I described my experience to my mom, she said it sounded just like she remembered it. Everyone that I had a chance to meet that day was so nice. That's a good thing considering the difficult situations that most of the young girls are in when they arrive. While the visit was eye opening, it added more perplexity to the questions already in my mind. Why would God fearing parents send their young daughter away to deal with this unplanned pregnancy on her own? As if the rape itself wasn't punishment enough, it seemed as if she was being punished again for something over which she absolutely had no control. When I asked my grandma why she sent my mother to the home, she said that was the advice she received from the local hospital. I guess with a deceased granddad and an aging grandma, I have to accept the reality that I may never get a direct answer that pleases me.

The plan was for her to stay there until my birth and then she would give me up for adoption. Thankfully this didn't go as planned. After my birth, she was determined to keep me. She didn't want to wonder where I was or if I was being taken care of properly. My grandmother, who is usually emotionless, had strong feelings about this as well. She told my mom that she didn't have to give me up for adoption which gave my mom the reassurance that she needed.

My mom never knew her rapist. I often wondered if she ever saw a man on the street and tried searching his face to see if his eyes looked familiar. I guess I've wondered this because so many times that's exactly what I did. I've always imagined that he's been close, watching me as I grew up, secretly being proud of my accomplishments but too afraid to admit to his wrong doing. However, I let go of those bullshit dreams a long time ago. If he ever appeared, I wouldn't kill him. But I don't spend time focusing on who he is, where he is or if he's proud of my accomplishments or not. What I know for sure is that my mom has always been present and remains one of my biggest cheerleaders.

For the most part, I had a pretty good childhood. Outside of getting peed on by my younger cousin each night, I don't have the sad childhood story of struggle that sells most personal testimonies. Also in the home were my three uncles. We were crowded, but we always had food to eat. I never remember being hungry or not having my basic needs met. As a matter of fact, I often wonder how my mom as a young parent, managed to be such a huge part of my life consistently. I was very active as a child, participating in activities that many other children, even in two-parent households, weren't able to participate. I was in dance, baton twirling, drama and gymnastics just to name a few activities. Sometimes I'm amazed at how responsible my mom was despite the way I came into existence. She was my biggest supporter for every activity in which I was involved. My mom was also my biggest supporter when I believed I was too skinny, too black and my hair was too nappy to be considered pretty. She would always remind me that the blacker the berry, the sweeter the juice, and would say, "When the berries are light they have no use."

When I was in the eleventh grade, my mom's continuous confidence boosting began to show in my actions. I truly began to believe I was the shit! It was also around this time that I began to believe that it must be some type of divine plan for me to be here on earth. Of course, I had no clue about the details of the plan. I dabbled in promiscuity. What a lie! The *naked* truth is that I dove into promiscuity head first. Although I wouldn't categorize my first sexual experience as traumatic, I was five years old and it was with a female family member. The feeling she gave me was one that I began to crave from that point. Masturbating and 'playing' with other girls was my drug of choice until losing my virginity at sixteen. Since that time I have had sex with a lot of men. I am not at all bragging about this fact, but it's a truth that I have chosen to be honest about instead of living in shame. I was never diagnosed with a sex addiction but I remember chasing the high that I felt whenever I was with someone new. I remember craving the new personality, the new body and the difference my body would feel in a new sexual experience. I remember creating a list of men I desired and then adding them to my list of accomplished conquests. There were times that I had sex with more than one new man in a week, sometimes two in one night.

Men became something I desired to conquer and the physical appearance that I had once questioned was now what I worshipped. As a result of my body image worshipping, I ended up dancing in a local strip club while I was in college. Although stripping is widely celebrated now as a cool thing to do, in the early 1990s it wasn't something about which one bragged. During that time, being a stripper was equated to being a hoe, being dirty or being *stank*. Therefore it was definitely something about which I kept quiet. Only those closest to me knew what I was doing. Although they were probably not that happy about it, they knew me well enough to know that I had my own mind, and they might as well keep their opinions to themselves.

I was pretty popular in high school. I went to college completely paid with scholarships. I partied way too much though and eventually dropped out, got pregnant and had a baby. Although leaving college sounds like I made a bad choice, considering I was making bad decisions in college, coming home probably saved my life. In college, I sold my textbooks for money to buy marijuana and alcohol. I once held a gun to a girl's head and pulled the trigger. Thankfully, the gun jammed and I didn't have to face a life in prison. Leaving college and subsequently having my first daughter was the universe's way of steering me in the right direction.

Being a former stripper who was promiscuous, drank and did drugs is also what drove my desire to stand in the church pulpit to announce to anyone that would listen that I had been changed. Jesus had called me to preach the gospel and declare the good news. I needed to declare to everyone that He was able and that it was by his grace that I no longer lived a life of sin. Looking back, it was about ten years from the time I had been an exotic dancer to the time of my initial sermon. I had changed, but I couldn't give Jesus the credit. I stopped stripping years prior to my desire to preach simply because it was something in which I was no longer interested. I began to see myself in a better light, and I wanted to make better decisions. I realized I could still embrace my sexiness without shaking my ass for strangers. Perhaps even then the universe was leading me to live a *naked* life, but I gravitated to the common meaning. I certainly wasn't at a place in my life to have any other epiphany. Then I hopped on "Thunder Road." Most people call it marriage. It was eleven years of intense boot camp that created the soldier I am today. The lessons I learned during that time are priceless, and I appreciate my ex-husband and the life we shared.

My life experiences have taught me more than I could have ever learned in a classroom. I wouldn't categorize any of these experiences as good or bad. They are just that…experiences. Most importantly, these experiences are responsible for shaping and molding me and I'm grateful for each of them. Instead of labeling experiences as good or bad, the best approach is to ask the question, "Did I learn something?"

Chapter 2 Naked Nuggets:

1. STAND IN YOUR TRUTH

Many times we can be embarrassed about where we come from. I on the other hand have completely embraced the person I used to be. This person played a big role in molding and shaping who I am today. The person I am right now will have a huge impact on the person I am in the future. Why lie? Whatever happened to you is in the past. Any dumb mistakes made are in your past. Every experience you have ever had influenced today's outcome. Embrace every part of you...good, bad or indifferent.

2. LOVE YOURSELF

If you don't love you, who will? I'm sure there were some people that laughed at me when I said I wanted to write a book. However, whether they purchase it or not is really none of my concern. I know I have something to say that is beneficial to a lot of people. You should always be the biggest investor in yourself and your own number one fan.

3. DON'T BE SO HARD ON YOURSELF

Learn to laugh at yourself and have fun. No one really likes to be around people who constantly have a stick in their ass!

Chapter 3

◆◇◆

SET YOUR BULLSHIT LIMIT!

"When you know someone is serving you bullshit, get up from the table."

Setting your bullshit limit is the first step that must be mastered before moving any further in life. As long as I was full of shit, people were attracted to me like flies! I've noticed that many of my acquaintances loved me as long as I was wandering around aimlessly. They wanted me to be the life of the party, keep them entertained with my dance skills and turn a blind eye to the lies we were all living. That was actually when I had the most 'friends'. However, as soon as I began to awaken and the lights came on, they scattered like roaches. If I could, I would pop a middle finger up right off of this page to them for not keeping it *naked*! But in all actuality, there was certainly a point when I wasn't even being real with myself. As I look back over my life, there were so many times that I altered things about myself to be accepted by those I admired. If I was told that I shouldn't wear dresses above my ankles, I didn't wear dresses above my ankles. If I thought dressing like an outdated lady in a brightly colored sequined suit with the hat to match made me look holier, that's what I wore. Anytime I wasn't being true to myself by catering to the needs of others, I became someone who attracted people who made a career out of living a charade. The statement "You attract what you are" is so very true. I was fake and therefore surrounded by fake people. Anytime I deviated from their plan for my life, I realized their professed unconditional love did in fact have conditions. I've found, after years of tap dancing for a coin in my bucket, that it is just easier to be who I am. People will always have something to say. However, if they don't like how you're living your life, there is only one solution for them and that's to…get the hell on! Some people believe they have the right to give you their unsolicited opinions. They can somehow magically see what's best for your life and get upset if you disagree with them. I have no problem disagreeing with them, and I'll even go as far as correcting someone if they try to say anything about my life that doesn't line up with my vision. I'll cut them off in the middle of their sentence if they try feeding me bullshit. Guarding your heart and ears is also part of setting the bullshit limit.

On more than one occasion, I've been disrespected by the words that people allow to flow from their mouths concerning me. I was always taught that life and death are in the power of the tongue. Some people have shortened the meaning of that truth to the phrase "Speak life." I learned that in church and when it comes to the Bible I can only say, "Don't throw the baby out with the bath water." There's some great advice listed in the Bible which is why I reference it often. It's the perfect book from which to gain knowledge as most of the information is gathered from other world religions. But again, I digress. As a writer, I've always known that words have the ability to be persuasive and invoke strong emotion. I must admit however that until recently, I wasn't aware of the life I've created for myself through the power of words. Because of this new awareness, I have begun to politely but insistently refuse to allow anyone to speak negativity into my life in my presence. I won't even listen to that bullshit!

I can remember having a conversation about relationships with a former coworker. The coworker told me that I should date a particular guy even though he wasn't attractive in my eyes because he would probably treat me right. However, because I remained persistent about my position, this person attempted to speak all manner of evil until I matter of factly began to speak affirmations directly against what this person was saying. As a result, I was told I take things too seriously. When it comes to my life, it is very serious! I think we should all be more mindful of the life we create for ourselves with our words. I don't like to hear people say things like, "If it's not one thing, it's another," or "If it wasn't for bad luck, I wouldn't have any luck at all." I especially don't like when they look to me to cosign foolish speaking. I refuse to let anyone create my tomorrow by the words I allow to be spoken about me or the statements with which I disagree. I encourage everyone to watch their words and begin to shape a more positive life for themselves beginning with what they think, followed by what they say. However, as the old saying goes, "You can lead a horse to water, but you can't make it drink."

I cannot control what's said when I'm not around. But I can definitely correct someone when I hear words being spoken with which I don't agree. I will not nod my head in agreement, say I understand, or just keep silent out of fear of offending. Some may say I take things too seriously, but I will continue to reject and correct anything that might negatively affect me even if it's just my mood. If you're easily offended be sure to come correct when I'm around or be prepared to be corrected. In other words, watch your mouth concerning me. I have a bullshit limit and it will certainly cost you if you go beyond it!

Keep in mind that as you start to have standards in certain areas, people may become uncomfortable and begin to walk away or avoid you. Initially, we may feel the sting of rejection. We may even shed a tear or two. Eventually, we must tap into our higher self and just get over it. As long as you know you have given your best, be okay with allowing the chips to fall where they may. Simply put two tears in a bucket. Understand that you may just be too much for them to handle. To the simpleton stiff necks that will reply "We aren't animals and don't need to be handled." You know what the hell I mean! Don't entertain the spirit of low self-esteem or low self-worth that can creep in when you try to rationalize why someone can't see you for who you really are. I've just come to accept that sometimes the mask that they wear is obstructing their vision. They are the ones missing out. While we should all evolve and change for the better, I'm not changing to pacify phoniness and neither should you. Be completely comfortable with accepting the blame for dissolved relationships between you and masquerading participants. Stop questioning and/or chasing people. Set your bullshit limit and stick to it by any means necessary!

Chapter 3 Naked Nuggets:

1. FREE YOURSELF FROM THE OPINIONS OF PEOPLE

Leave your life in the hands of others and you will never get a chance to live. The truth is, you most definitely won't ever be able to please everyone. Some people will support the choices you make in life and others will constantly express their disappointment. If you alter who you are to try to please people, you will find yourself in a state of schizophrenia.

2. WATCH YOUR WORDS

I am always amazed at the amount of people that get so offended by four letter words. I've been *unfriended* on social media for using shit, damn, hell, etc. I've also heard people say that using four letter words makes one sound unintelligent. However, these same people create lives of negativity for themselves by all of the so called clean foolishness they utter. Watch the bullshit that you allow to flow from your mouth that's seeping from your inner being.

3. DON'T BE AFRAID TO DISAGREE

Disagreement doesn't always have to be a place of contention. It's okay not to agree with someone when they are looking to you to accept their lies about you. For example, when asked "Don't you feel like every time you get ahead, something snatches you back?" There's nothing wrong with replying "Nope, I can't say that I do." Avoid cosigning with negativity. This is your life and it is definitely that serious!

Chapter 4

◆◇◆

RELIGION

"Organized religion is for dummies."

"Cut the crap (feces, dung)! Get rid of the foolishness! God will not bring more members into this feces filled church if they have to watch their step!" The church was charged and those that enjoy a good hard message cheered me forward. This was one of the last sermons I preached from the pulpit in the church where I was an ordained Associate Minister. I had preached my initial sermon just eight years earlier. Although I grew up in the church, the last eight years had been filled with a voracious appetite for the word of God. I definitely hadn't been perfect but more often than not, I was extremely concerned with *what Jesus would do* and/or what God would do *to* me; either on this side or in the afterworld. I appeared to be confident and strong, except maybe when I was at the altar crying over marital problems. I was actually sinking, drowning in my own misery because I was lost and unhappy with living the life of a puppet. It's no coincidence that the "Religion" chapter follows the "Set Your Bullshit Limit" chapter. I had spent the last eight years trying to be all things to all people. I wanted to be that Bible believing, prayer warrior that everyone idolized. I had the role of a righteous, church going woman down pat. I didn't smoke, drink, listen to secular music or wear revealing clothes. I sat in judgment of those that didn't seem to have it as together as I thought I did. To add Christian icing to the cake, I spent most of my time in church. I was that person that many say is so heavenly minded that they're no earthly good. Don't get me wrong, growing up in a local C.M.E church spawned some of my greatest memories.

GROWING UP IN CHURCH

Normally, pastors are assigned to different churches on a rotation. This meant we got to meet a new family with new kids to play with every few years. This greatness was combined with the fact that most of the church families were fixed community members who as a result, were also long standing church members. This meant that no matter what school you attended, your church friends remained the same. Parents didn't have to second guess the safety of play dates with church members because nine times out of ten, they had known the family for years. There was also limited worry of anyone being misled religiously by our friends since we all went to the same church, or at least believed in the same God.

I was very active in church as a child. I was a member of the missionary circles. I sang in the children's and youth choirs and then briefly in the choir for young adults. I was a part of the junior usher board and the Christian Youth Fellowship (C.Y.F). I attended Vacation Bible School as far back as I can remember, and as a teen I was an active member of the youth Bible study class. All of these groups came with many activities and the opportunity to meet other youth that had the same beliefs as me.

Of all the church activities in which I participated, I think the junior usher board had to be the worst one. Although we took a trip every summer to a nearby amusement park, our advisor, in my opinion, was a strict, mean, old lady. She seemed to have no empathy for my weak little legs. I hated having to stand up for the majority of the service in that ugly gabardine outfit with that god awful thick white collar that was attached by safety pins. It also seemed pointless to stand in the aisle as if we were really in charge of seating; most of the regular members sat in the same spot Sunday after Sunday. God forbade someone else was in their spot, there was hell to pay! God forbade you would try to sit some of those evil witches anywhere else. On top of all that, no one took the time to teach me not to lock my knees. So every fourth Sunday, I would stand in the aisle light headed and trying not to faint. I was probably somewhat self-conscious as well; especially if I had failed to put activator in my Jheri curl or if it was time for a re-touch. My pantyhose sagged around my thin Olive Oyl legs and itched like crazy. I wasn't able to scratch until we were summoned by Evilene to sit down. This was always right before a dry sermon that I could never understand. As a matter of fact, there was only one lady that seemed to agree with the pastor, and she could be heard over anyone else yelling with a southern drawl, "Yeessss, Amen!" I can't remember at what age I was finally able to quit the Junior Usher Board, but I'm sure I celebrated.

I think the children's choir rehearsed two Tuesdays out of the month, and we shared the second Sunday with the youth choir. Perhaps we had more than one children's choir director, but only one stands out in my head. She had really big bright teeth and she was always smiling. She was so sweet. Then there was our dedicated pianist. Our pastors weren't known for a lot of whooping and hollering, so the pianist wasn't needed to add musical effects to the sermon. I actually think he would leave during this time to take a smoke break outside with the other male smokers of the church. Singing in the choir was quite fun though except when I was given a lead part that just never seemed to sound right on Sunday mornings. In my mind I could sing, in my room at home I could sing, but at church...I couldn't sing. I also remember traveling to the nursing homes, especially around Christmas time to sing Christmas carols and pass out tissue. Thank God that during these times we would sing as a group. As we know the elderly are known for saying exactly what's on their minds. Although singing at the nursing homes was a nice gesture, I always hated being around old people and didn't want them to touch me. Most of them didn't have any teeth and more often than not, they would have food oozing from the corners of their mouths. Sometimes we would travel to sing at other churches. We would have so much fun singing on the van ride there and back home. As a member of the children's choir, I also remember wishing I was old enough to be in the youth choir. That's where the cute boys and cool church girls were. Not that I would've ever gotten a second look because dark skin wasn't in back then. The youth choir had also made an album; making them local celebrities within the church and community. Finally, I turned thirteen and was able to join the youth choir! I took my pencil legs and broken off hair, damaged from switching from a curl to a relaxer, proudly into my new group. This change brought on another choir director.

Although she wasn't as mild mannered, she was just as sweet and fun. Under her direction, we even won a local singing competition.

Because church was always extremely fun, I never had a problem being there. It always seemed like one never ending social event. Church advisors kept us busy with fun activities. I can still remember an activity in Vacation Bible School designed to teach us about faith. We had to be blind folded and completely trust our teacher to take care of us as she dropped something strange in our mouths. Thankfully, they were only chocolate covered gummy worms. Everything about Vacation Bible School was fun from the art, music, and recreational activities to preparing a magnificent presentation for the last day. There was never a dull moment with church. If we weren't going out to eat, we were headed to the local skating rink, movie theater or some other exciting event. I would also attend annual church conferences with my grandma each summer which meant more socializing. While the adults were caught up in meetings, we teenagers would roam the hotel acting as if we were grown.

Hands down, growing up in the church gave me some of the best times I've ever had. Every Sunday my friends and I would sit on the second to the last row in church idolizing the high school teens that would walk across the street to the store before service. They would snack and chat the entire time. I knew that eventually I'd be old enough to walk to the store and sit on the back row too. I loved my church so much that I would even bring friends along that grew attached to the church through Vacation Bible School and teen Bible study. Our charismatic teen Bible study teachers even led us to make our own informed decision to accept Jesus Christ and be baptized.

Being a member of the missionary circles represent my most favorite times with the church. It was with these groups that I had a chance to travel and participate in summer retreats. Those retreats allowed me one week away from home each summer and gave me a break from my younger cousin, who had the nerve to expect me to actually share with her. Of course, this was also the time when I began to learn that everyone in church wasn't trying to live according to the Bible. Although teenagers will be teenagers, it was the church teens that taught me what it actually meant for a girl to be *fingered*. I also learned that some girls have a very identifiable but not always pleasant smell. Nevertheless, those were happy times. Lifetime memories were made along the way with lifetime acquaintances. I still look forward to visiting my home church on Anniversary Day or Family and Friends Day hoping that I run into those childhood friends.

I'm sure that most of us that grew up in my home church share many of the same memories and the warm fuzzy feelings. We would be hard pressed to forget the chewing gum lady, the lady whose hair was three different colors, the musician that we thought looked like a bird, the star singers and which older ladies made the best potato salad, cornbread or macaroni and cheese. Fellow church members were like family. Church is where I met Ms. Shirley. She was a beautiful young adult that did hair out of her kitchen. Every hair service was only twenty dollars. She played a pivotal role during my senior year in high school by helping me to feel beautiful and comfortable with the way I looked as I started to develop. At twenty years old when I was unwed and pregnant by a married man, it was Ms. Shirley that called me on the phone with encouraging words. I clearly remember feeling encouraged and less ashamed as she said, "Shemeka, you aren't the first young lady to have a baby out of wedlock and you won't be the last!"

I enjoyed my home church so much that I continued to attend well into adulthood even after I became a mom. Then things begin to change. I begin to see more and hear more and have more questions. It was very hard to see people that I looked to as examples live double lives. I couldn't understand how an active church member was having an illicit relationship with another woman's husband. I couldn't understand why the same members year after year seemed to have so much control. It never sat right with me when I experienced rude behavior from members that were leaders in the church. I've heard sayings such as "Keep your eyes on God because humans will be humans." However, these behaviors were unacceptable to me. These questions would send me on a search that would lead me to four different churches within ten years resulting in my current non-attending state. It also led me to embark on my own personal spiritual journey.

CHURCH AS AN ADULT

Going to church on New Year's Eve for watch night service had been a tradition for me since high school. Even if I left the service and went to the club, there was no way I would bring in the New Year in any other place. I had also started a tradition of having a few friends and family members over on New Year's Eve for some of my delicious homemade lasagna. Since church didn't start until ten o'clock this was never a conflict and we all looked forward to it. This particular New Year's Eve, my mom, grandma, aunt and uncle were present. One of my good friends, who lived in the apartment right below me, came up as well. My best friend was there with her boyfriend; they were expecting a baby. We all ate, sat around, laughed and just enjoyed our time together. My best friend and I attended the same church and we both wanted our boyfriends to attend service with us. For the first time in years, I was in a real relationship. I wanted him to attend service because I was also very superstitious. My grandma had always said whatever you were doing when the new year came in, that's what you would be doing all year. Since I was in a relationship that I was hoping would last forever,

I really wanted us to bring the New Year in together. That would mean we would stay together at least for the next year.

Unfortunately my boyfriend Kareem (My ex-husband didn't want his name in this book. Therefore, moving forward, he'll be referred to as Kareem) wasn't that interested in church. He had attended another local church as a child. Presently, he believed that it wasn't necessary to go to church. He believed that no matter what they had done, all black people were going to heaven. He also wasn't interested in attending my church because the pastor at the time was extremely boring. He told the same old boring Bible stories that we had all heard before, the same old boring way. He also talked with a twang that was difficult to understand. On top of that he dressed like a washed up pimp. I definitely couldn't fault my boyfriend for not being interested. However, it was the church I grew up in and I couldn't stray from normal tradition. Going to church on New Year's Eve was a tradition and I wasn't willing to break it. Even if I did attend church, come home and have premarital sex, I was going. My best friend and I finally persuaded our boyfriends to attend church with us that night. We were all hopeful that this guest pastor would be able to say something that we actually understood and hold our attention. We had no clue as to how much of a treat we were about to receive.

The pastor's praise team of about four people opened the service. It wasn't the usual dry hymns or rehearsed songs that I was used to hearing. I can still remember his wife belting out "Hell is deep and hell is wide, but hell ain't got no joy inside!" We were on our feet enjoying the singing like never before. In fact, it seemed like all of the people the guest pastor brought with him were young adults. I was amazed to see young people actually looking like they were enjoying church. From the time the guest pastor took the microphone until he sat down, I was intrigued. I sat completely engrossed by his words. He preached with such conviction and I was captivated by the words that were coming from his mouth. He spoke with such simplicity; I was finally learning something in church at twenty-five years old.

After church, life went on as usual. We ate the breakfast that was always served after watch night service, and then we went home and had premarital sex just as I knew we would. When Sunday rolled around, my boyfriend actually suggested that we attend the home church of the guest preacher at the New Year's Eve service. I had never missed a Sunday service at my home church to attend another church. However, I was so excited that he wanted to go to church, that I was happy to accompany him.

This was the most exciting service I had ever attended. The music was good and the preaching was even better. It was also quite entertaining. It was the typical storefront church, and I witnessed everything I had been told about this kind of church. The women had on dresses that went down to their ankles and the men seemed to be in charge. When the *spirit was high*, some of them broke out in a dance that looked as if something had taken control of their bodies. Others took off running around the church and speaking in a strange unintelligible language. A man stood by the pulpit reading from the Bible and was also there, when instructed by the pastor, to wipe a drop of sweat if need be. The church was small with only a few members, but everyone was so friendly; it instantly felt like family. Once the service ended, we were greeted with a lot of affection. It was as if they were sincerely excited to have us there. One of the female members that appeared to be around my age asked for my phone number. They collectively made sure that we knew they wanted us to come back again. Kareem even expressed how much he enjoyed himself and stated that if he was going to attend church on Sundays, that church was the church he wanted to attend.

I never went back to my home church, at least not as a full-time member. We felt so at home in the new church that we continued to attend Sunday after Sunday. Kareem even decided to join one Sunday when the pastor 'opened up the doors' of the church for membership. I knew then that I had the choice to join the church as well or end up with us attending two different churches. I wasn't willing to let that happen, especially since there was one particular single woman in the church that was obviously a man hungry vulture. It was almost as if she was constantly circling and waiting on the most opportune time to swoop in on her prey. She was the same one that asked for my number the first day we visited, and she was always inquiring about the details of my intimate relationship with

Kareem. She had been married once, was divorced and acted as if she had all of the answers. She seemed to be a very important part of the ministry.

The next two months were a great religious experience. After being in the church all of my life, I learned that Pontius Pilate was a man. I could recite the books of the Bible and was beginning to memorize scriptures. Going to church was never boring because there were other couples there that were my age. They were young, married, raising children and dedicated Christians, models of what I wanted for my life.

Church was like an addiction. I was there every time the doors opened. I stopped drinking and hanging out with my friends. In Matthew 12:49, Jesus refers to his disciples as his mother and brother. He considered his family to be those with whom he worshipped. Therefore, if someone didn't attend my church, I wouldn't hang around them because, in my opinion, they weren't living up to the standards of the Bible. I slowly drifted away from friends that I had known since childhood. The same friends that I had so much fun with at my home church, started to hear less and less from me. What made it even easier to walk away from these friends was that my friend, who lived in the apartment right under me, joined the same church. Once again, church was like a big social event that I never wanted to miss. The biggest difference between this church and the one I grew up in was that I actually felt like God was pleased because I was really learning *his word* and trying to live by it.

Living by *his* word meant getting married to the man that I was already living with since fornication was a sin. At this point, we weren't having sex or sleeping in the same bed and it was hard. According to 1 Thessalonians 5:22, we are instructed to "abstain from the appearance of evil" so we didn't even want someone to think we were doing wrong by the way things looked. Kareem asked me to marry him in April of that year. Initially, we chose to get married in September. However, due to pressure from the church leaders, we married in June of that year. 1 Corinthians 7:9 informs us, "…it's better to marry than to burn with passion." Since Kareem and I didn't want to burn in *hell*, we wanted to do everything right. It was his idea to move up the date. I thought it was simply because he could see how serious I was about obeying God's word.

It was that or he was tired of sleeping in a twin bed and wanted to have sex. We married in June and that's when all hell broke loose.

I have mixed feelings about getting married when we did. As stated before, I believe that every experience is just that, an experience. It's neither good nor bad and experience is needed for growth. However, the timing of our marriage and getting married primarily for religious reasons made it a very difficult marriage to endure. Kareem remained the same, but my newfound commitment to Christianity had changed everything about me. The way I thought and responded to certain situations, the way I dressed and even how I celebrated holidays changed. For instance, every year my home church held a Halloween carnival complete with a haunted house. However, in this new church, we were taught that Halloween was of the devil. Therefore, I stopped taking my daughter, five at the time, trick-o-treating. Instead, we celebrated Hallelujah night. Our church family got together, sat around and mimicked each other in the way we danced and ran around the church during services. I became so judgmental. Having a conversation with me was like talking with a speaking

Bible. I loved learning scriptures. Not just so that I would know how to live and how not to live, but also for ammunition when I needed to put people in their place about their raggedy lifestyle. I was what some Christians call "on fire for Jesus" which by the way, is the dumbest shit I've ever heard. What I actually had, was zeal with no knowledge, or rather 'limited' knowledge because it was all based on one book, The Holy Bible.

Hindsight is twenty-twenty, and now I can see the bondage I was in although I was blind to it then. I would never wear shorts and more often than not, skirts or dresses came down to my ankles. I laugh when I think about what I must've looked like in my rhinestone suit with matching hat singing the words "There's a leak in this old building." My goal was to have a suit in every color so Kareem and I could dress alike just like the pastor and his first lady. I wouldn't listen to any secular (non-Christian) music, not even in the bedroom. After such an exciting sex life while we were dating, religious beliefs made us both dull and boring in bed. Attending church was all I wanted to do. From selling fish dinners, second services on Sundays, to weekday services scheduled just to raise offerings, I spent most of my time at church. Any free time was also spent with those same church members. After all, I no longer had any friends outside of that church. On the 9th day of June 2002, I preached my initial sermon and was licensed as an evangelist. The church was packed, filled with supporters as well as those that were trying to determine if I was in a cult. I preached what was known in church jargon as a hard sermon. That is a sermon that's straight to the point and sometimes tough to receive because it isn't sugarcoated. The church was in an uproar and I received praise for a job well done from not only my pastor, but pastors of other churches that were present. I knew I had been called to guide people and I thought that preaching was the way. I served the church with everything in me, even during Kareem's short stint in prison. We stayed several more months after his release from prison. However, the way the church was handling finances and what we considered to be a poverty mentality, we decided to leave that church only to join a bigger church with the same mentality.

The new church had even more man hungry women. From the very beginning, I found out who was cheating with whose husband, who had divorced who to marry someone else, sometimes only to go back to the previous spouse. Sound like a lot? It was. This church was aesthetically nicer and had many more members. So there were more people running, jumping and shouting and much more space to do it. The pastor was a boisterous female with a raspy voice, and I was immediately in love with her style of teaching and preaching. However, this was the worst church experience I've ever had. I was pregnant, lost in the sauce and had no real friends there. What I didn't realize at the time was that this church would play an intricate part in teaching me or helping me to see what I hated about religion. This is probably when I began to feel like organized religion was for dummies because I was feeling quite ridiculous. I had never seen so many people move throughout life like programmed robots. The real intelligence of people rarely peaked through as most of the members moved about and acted the same. Before long, I was trying my best to fit in although I never really did. The best part was that every Sunday I had the opportunity to do one of the things that I absolutely love doing, dancing. I was also a part of the choir. Both of these activities gave me an opportunity to get out of the house at least twice a week. I had fallen into the mundane role of the stay at home housewife. However, I would only continue to lose myself as I sat in a church surrounded by people full of greed and jealousy. You would think that the greed mentality of almost every member would've spawned at least one millionaire. Instead, it only perpetuated the poverty mentality that so many of them had. They lived pay check to pay check while hopelessly waiting on the Lord for a breakthrough. That church almost exemplified the crab in the barrel syndrome. Except, instead of other crabs trying to pull down the crab showing potential, the crab that showed potential, voluntarily remained in the barrel destined to go nowhere.

The next church I attended was led by husband and wife that were former youth pastors of the previous church. This shows how blind I was, to think that I would actually have a dramatically different experience with the same people. While I certainly believe that this church was more organized, it was destined to fail. Along with some of the members, the pastors practiced the same church politics and policies that made the previous church so dysfunctional. Outside of the negative points I noted, this church wasn't so bad. We had great family rapport. One of the most positive things that came from this experience is that I was given more room to find myself and exercise my true passions. It was at this church that I was ordained as an Associate Minister. This had been a long time coming considering I was originally licensed in 2002. I had opportunities to preach on Sundays, to teach Bible study on Wednesday nights, to lead the dance ministry and to sing on the praise team. However, even with all of this involvement, I still felt as if I was missing something. I remember sitting in church on many occasions as if I were an outsider looking in, watching the service like it was a movie. Every Sunday we did the same rituals. Between praise, worship and the sermon, the majority of the church would bounce around looking like fools to the sound of war themed music. Today, I can't help but ask myself just what in the hell we were fighting and why were we fighting. It never failed, Sunday after Sunday, the pastor and his wife would lead us in an emotionally charged service. This happened every Sunday, despite most members, including myself, leaving afterwards to face grim realities and defeated lives. We looked good doing it though. We were always well dressed, wearing our best clothes with the best weaves.

This time of my life was probably the most depressing. My marriage was cracking like glass and I had no idea who Shemeka Michelle was or even why she was put on this earth at this point. I swayed back and forth from thinking God didn't want me to be miserable to thinking this was the cup I had been given and I had to drink from it. Although I was running, shouting, speaking in tongues, singing, preaching, teaching and living upright, it seemed that Jesus refused to fix my marriage. To many, it would seem as if my current state of not attending church is based on the disappointment of my marriage and church hurt. To me, the phrase 'church hurt' is really just lame church jargon used to guilt people into returning to the church instead of seeking truth. The reality, however, was that my marriage couldn't be fixed by any outside force. My frustration with church continued to grow. I knew my time at this church was limited. I watched people placed in positions based on popularity and grew weary of participating in foolish acts. I no longer enjoyed participating in what now seemed like a religious circus, performing for people who only came week after week to be entertained. I knew there was more to life than this. I truly believed I was missing something although I was yet to figure out what that something was.

My last attempt to be part of a church congregation was probably one of the best experiences. It was a predominately white church that refrained from the theatrics that irritated me. The pastor and his wife didn't have their pictures plastered all over the building. There were no seats reserved for special members of the church, and I didn't hear members referring to one another with lengthy titles. I later found out that they had even allowed an atheist to serve in a pseudo leadership position. He eventually gave his life to Christ as a result of the love that he had experienced. Although for the most part, everyone was extremely nice, I felt out of place and out of touch with black people because my children and I were the only black family in the congregation at the time. If there was a heaven, I was certain that it wasn't segregated and I couldn't understand why it was so hard to find a church that wasn't separated by race. Aside from the racial disparity, I continued to feel like something was missing. I couldn't shake the sense that I was still far from the truth. I wasn't content with believing that anyone who didn't accept Jesus as their personal savior was condemning themselves to an eternity of hellfire. Nothing in my deepest being understood or agreed with that.

LEAVING RELIGION

As I started my journey to remove the masks I had been wearing, it turned out that organized religion was one of them. The scripture John 8:36 says that, "Who the Son sets free is free indeed," but I didn't feel free. I still felt disconnected to what I believed to be God. I was bound by the rules of man. I didn't like that feeling. It didn't feel genuine. However, at the time, I didn't have much information to back up why I was feeling this way. All I knew was the Bible. I had been taught from birth that these sixty-six books were the infallible word of God. I had believed for so long that if I didn't live my life according to what was in that book, I was sure to burn in hell. None of this felt right to me. As I would gaze up at the stars at night, the infinity of the universe made me feel that everything I had learned was absolute nonsense. Therefore I set out on a mission to find truth and peace.

I began to read and study, research and study some more. When people say, "The rabbit hole goes deep," they aren't lying. While I believe that there is something greater than us that connects everything, I believe that there is no one religion that could encompass that vast greatness. In fact, religion has done nothing but create separation, appealing to the egotistical side of humans that make them feel the need to be different and therefore think themselves better than others. Christianity is one of the most violent and hateful religions outside of so called devil worship. Does this mean that I believe that all Christians are evil people, not at all! I simply believe that there is enough historical evidence to suggest that Christianity is built on lies and deceit. Most people are afraid to research these topics for fear of damnation. I was even told by a Christian that I shouldn't open myself up to confusion by trying to learn. Using that logic, I guess the only way to be a good Christian is to have blind faith and not ask any questions even if certain things don't make sense to you. I was tired of hearing "God's ways are not our ways and his thoughts are higher than our thoughts." That only screamed to me "Sit down, shut up and remain disconnected from all that is." That certainly wasn't going to work for me.

Amazingly, leaving the church seemed to bring me closer to God than I had ever experienced. I began to believe that God was all and in all and I do mean all! I could no longer find solace in rejecting people simply because they had a different concept of God. After all, every religion's ideology is based on a concept. This played a huge role in my life as I began to remove the mask I had been wearing. It was also a very beneficial outlook to have as I began to blog, connecting with people from all walks of life. I no longer allowed beliefs to separate me from someone or hinder my ability to recognize the life experiences that we shared. I needed to think a new way in order to help people. I began to see God in everything from people to trees to birds. Some people refer to what I call God as a higher being, source of energy, the universe or all that is. Regardless to what reference one chooses to use, I have a deeper sense of self because of this concept. I no longer need a rule book to guide me because the deepest part of me is now connected to all that is. This principle combined with love and appreciation is what guides me day to day.

Chapter 4 Naked Nuggets:

1. KNOW THYSELF

Who are you without the confines of religion? Are you so out of touch with your innermost being that you can only function according to manmade rules? Can you exercise compassion without these rules? Can you love because you allow what's on the inside of you to flow outwardly? If you move, live and experience life based on the unfounded belief in someone or something other than yourself, you do not know thyself.

2. FOLLOW YOUR HEART

When everyone else stops talking, you can hear your heart speak. Your heart will never lead you to anger, division or hate. At the end of the day, you may have to stand alone but at least you'll be standing with someone you can trust.

3. THOU SHALT NOT TELL A LIE, WEAR A MASK OR PRETEND

Why? Simply because I'm sick of that shit! 1Nakedlonians 4:3

Chapter 5

◆◇◆

<u>DATING 101</u>

Never lose yourself trying to find someone else.
~Unknown~

Truth is……. Some of you will NEVER have a mate. That's the harsh reality that many refuse to tell you. It isn't the universe's way of punishing you either. Some of you will be single forever simply because you refuse to be open, honest and *naked*. You don't understand that when you are constantly living a lie, refusing to be who you really are, your relationships will always fail. This is because either your mate will wake up and realize you're a fraud, or the charade will begin to make you miserable. Being inauthentic is definitely a relationship killer.

Dating is in a category all its own because most of these occurrences never turn into relationships. However, a lot of you won't even date. How do you expect to get to know someone if you never spend any time together? And I'm not talking about over and over again, subjecting yourself to boring misery. I'm a firm believer that it doesn't take long once you're in someone's presence to recognize whether or not you want to be with that person again. I don't care if the person is nice and has a great man or woman résumé. If your personalities don't click or you don't like him or her, you just don't like him or her. But you will never know if you don't take time out of your busy schedule to see.

Also, some of you are just so uptight. Relax! Unless you don't have a sense of humor and you only have a serious side, it's okay to laugh on the first date. We waste too much time sending our representatives to dates instead of showing up ourselves. Don't get me wrong, I'm not saying you have to lay all of your cards on the table on the first date. Don't scare off the other person before he or she even gets the chance to know you. Ladies, perhaps you should refrain from showing you are completely jealous and deranged. Men, perhaps you should let the head above your neck take the spotlight. We all know the other head exists. No need to make it the central focus on your first date. But if you don't relax and be yourself, how will you know if you are really interested in seeing each other again? Sometimes, there are no second dates because the representative you sent to the first one was too stiff and stuffy. Many of you don't realize that your representative's personality actually sucks!

And for goodness sakes, on behalf of sweet baby Jesus and the rest of the world, please be honest. If you aren't interested in moving forward with the other person, just say so. Life is too short to have anyone waiting by the phone (not that anyone should) for a call you already know you will never make. If you are trying to place that person on the back burner just in case, you are already losing. It is okay to date until you find the person that you really like and want to see more. It's completely okay to be honest about that.

Another important factor in dating that will keep you from wasting your time is listening. Many of us simply don't listen. I refuse to believe that on a grand scale, people are out there just deceiving us while we're clueless. Many times we don't hear a person's real intentions because we talk too much and listen too little. What I noticed just recently is that a person will reveal their true desires early. At the start of my current relationship, I learned upfront that he wasn't interested in a woman that was involved with someone else. He wasn't into playing games, and he didn't want any drama in his life. He didn't rattle this off in our first conversation nor was he direct, but I was paying attention. I was listening to what he was saying and I heard him loud and clear.

Believe it or not, dating isn't rocket science. With so many relationship experts circling the globe, we've made it harder than it really is. Setting out on a quest to find a mate is really simple: be honest, know what you want, stick to it and follow your intuition. I'm so tired of hearing "I can't find a man/woman." For goodness sakes, be you and fucking find your person, or let them find you, whichever you prefer. No one really knows you better than you know yourself. If you don't know yourself, you have no business dating.

Many times we end up in dead end relationships because we go into relationships not knowing what we really want and also looking for the wrong shit. I have a friend who coined the phrase "dating on your level." It sounds so simple, but as I look at my relationships that have met their demise, it's clear that I didn't understand this concept. I have a daughter that's twenty years old. At the time of her conception, her father was married. Clearly he wasn't on my level because he wasn't single or emotionally available for what I thought I wanted in life. I should've known better and parts of me did. However, it didn't stop me from signing up to be the number two chick in her dad's life. Side chicks have been around since the beginning of time. Some women even claim to have found glory in being number two. My story however is a little different. As a side chick, I wasn't wined and dined or taken on any expensive shopping trips. It wasn't until after mind blowing sex and a strong emotional attachment, did I learn this handsome man was nine years my senior, married and the father of five children. Yes, one, two, three, four, five children!

Initially after finding this out, I took the stance that I would never settle for being second. However, I was twenty years old, naïve, hot in the pants and obviously way in over my head.

Although I knew it was wrong, I couldn't resist him when he called. After all, there was something special about me that he couldn't resist either; at least that's what I told myself. I had convinced myself that he wasn't receiving what he needed at home. As time passed, I grew more and more attached. He would come over after work each night. Initially, he would not stay all night. After sex, he would fall asleep and I would ignore my urge to scratch or even use the bathroom because I didn't want to wake him. I wanted him to stay with me all night and eventually he did. He started staying until about six in the morning, probably arriving home before his children woke up and realized dad wasn't home.

Imagine the fear and uncertainty that gripped my heart when the second line appeared on the home pregnancy test. Not only was I only twenty years old, I was completely clueless on how to raise a child. He convinced me that abortion was wrong and said he would never support it. He told me I had nothing to worry about and that I could trust him to be there for us. It never dawned on me that I couldn't trust this man who cheated on his wife, not to lie to me too. How could he be in two places at one time? How would he be able to be a father to his children that lived in his house and be there for our child too? The harsh reality was that he couldn't be in two places. He was never there for our child, and I don't think he ever intended to be.

Most women with any amount of self-worth would have learned from this experience. However, it wasn't until I was lying on the abortion table with tears streaming down my face terminating our second pregnancy did I realize I was worth more and I deserved better. Together we had created a beautiful daughter. But as this new life was being sucked out of me, it finally dawned on me that I would never be number one and we would never be a family. I was lost, broken hearted, alone and scared. My daughter grew up with a weak relationship with her father and her paternal side of the family. Although I have a daughter from the relationship that I wouldn't trade for anything, I wasted my time becoming involved with an attached man.

Dating on your level is more than just dating someone you have things in common with though. It's fabulous that you both like to Jet Ski. However if your outlook on life differs drastically, you may be in for trouble. This is my take on the "date on your level" phrase. Also, we often settle for people others choose for us instead of the person we really like. I have never understood why people feel like their opinions should be weighted in a relationship in which they are not involved. I've heard many say that the first time you marry for love, the second time you marry for money. I knew after my divorce that I couldn't follow that saying. Having boatloads of money never really meant much to me and I wasn't going to start judging a man on his wallet now. There was a song out in the 80's that women sang, "Ain't nothing going on but the rent." Although the rent was still going on in my life along with a car note, car insurance, cell phone, grooming needs, three girls and the list goes on, experience had taught me that money couldn't buy happiness. I'd had the relationship with a flashy, materialistic Puff Daddy type and I knew that wasn't what I was looking for anymore. A man with money was actually on my 'would be nice but not necessary' list. Don't get me wrong, I didn't want a bum. But dating on my level allowed me to know I needed something different. Besides, there is so much more to a good man than his paycheck. There is so much more to me than bills. Although I'm not a fan of *off* brands, I am not impressed with a man that determines his worth by the material things he owns. I have to look past his wallet, because in a world where plastic tits and asses rule everything around me, I need him to look past my average sized butt and saggy breasts.

Part of being honest in looking for a partner is also being *naked* about the fact that I want someone to which I am attracted. In my opinion this is one area we lie about a lot. I see nothing wrong with dating someone to which you are physically attracted. After all, if things work out, you're going to be looking at him or her every night and every morning. Why not be sure it's a face you can stomach? Before we even get to know someone's personality, we see him or her. If there's no physical attraction and you can barely stand looking at someone, why waste time? I'm really interested in a man's character and integrity, but I also want him to appeal to me physically. When he forgets to take out the trash or does something really ridiculous, I still want to look at him and be ready to rip off my panties because I think he's just that fine. I love the simple things in life. I don't care about money, power or fame. I'm satisfied with a good man who is willing to let me define myself and be a woman on my own terms. For some that is asking way too much but Mr. Right knows this is a necessity for me. Don't date and then enter into a relationship with someone that you're hoping you can mold into your perfect mate. Like the person for whom he or she is now.

Chapter 5 Naked Nuggets:

1. WRITE THREE LISTS AND STICK TO THEM

I think every single person should have a list. This list should include at least five must haves in a relationship, five things that would be nice but aren't necessary and five deal breakers. This list would be a constant reminder and serve as a guide to keep one from waking up and asking the question "How did I get here?" These lists would help us to weed out the weak links from the beginning.

2. GO WITH YOUR GUT

This should actually be number one. We were given natural instincts for a reason, yet many of us ignore the little voice in our head or feeling within that tries to guide us. Truthfully, we know whether or not someone is a good mate for us early in the relationship. However, we play stupid then end up looking stupid. Many times we refuse to read the writing on the wall. If the person you are dating is married or involved with someone else who doesn't know about you, chances are your mate isn't trustworthy.

3. DATE YOUR CHOICE NOT YOUR MAMA'S CHOICE

They are our relationships yet we give so many people a say in who we choose. This is mostly because we fail to practice Nugget number two. If we could learn to trust ourselves and be guided by our own inner being, we wouldn't rely on others so much to make such important decisions for us. Get to know yourself. Learn to trust yourself. Then choose who you want to go through life with for yourself!

Chapter 6

♦◊♦

RELATIONSHIPS

"If it doesn't work, get the hell out!"

As with any relationship, you have to watch out for the red flags and relationship killers and take heed when you see them. Most of us fail to do this time and time again. We end up in one dead end relationship after the other simply because we fail to pay attention and learn from our mistakes. One relationship red flag that I had to learn not to ignore was insecurity, defined as uncertainty or anxiety about oneself, or lack of confidence. This anxiety and lack of confidence can be transferrable in relationships. When you're in a relationship with a person that is insecure, a question as simple as "Where have you been?" can turn into an assault on your character. Being in a relationship with a person whose lack of confidence breeds unwarranted distrust is absolutely exhausting. If you aren't careful, your partner's lack of confidence becomes your lack of confidence. You begin to question everything about yourself. Sadly, this isn't as simple as second guessing your appearance or physical attributes. This insecurity can cause you to second guess and lose confidence in your very purpose for being.

This became all too real for me. I was in a relationship with a man who turned into a gnawing ankle biter that felt the need to rake over my character with a fine tooth comb. Although I had never cheated on him or had the desire to be with someone else, I could never do enough to prove this fact to him. I'm a people person and I love to share my life experiences with others. In order to do this, I must communicate with people. For him, this was always a problem because in his eyes, any man that even spoke to me only wanted to get in my panties. It never dawned on him that at his best, he cosigned my feeling of beauty internally and externally. I was happy with him. Another man's intentions for me should never have been a cause for mistrust. However, it never mattered that he was the only man I desired. I was constantly badgered by him, nearly stifling my very existence. He started to treat me as if I lacked the intelligence to make proper choices. How in the hell did he think he could question my intelligence? He constantly questioned my intentions as if I lacked any type of morals and values. We would literally have arguments over things that didn't even exist. It got to the point that I hated to be around him or even see his number on my caller ID. I attributed his bad behavior to feeling unworthy of my attention and affection. Why? Because he was insecure with who he was and what qualities he brought to the table. Every day I strapped on tap shoes preparing for the tiring dance to prove my love. Many of us have fallen for the lie that this type of obsessive behavior is a way of showing love. However, stunting your ability to flourish, grow and evolve isn't love. If you aren't careful, this can actually turn into a codependent, insecurity riddled relationship.

I'm a true believer that you have to separate a person's lack from his or her worth. Minor insecurities don't necessarily equate to deal breakers. After all, many things can contribute to one's lack of confidence and a lot of us have held minor anxieties about ourselves at one time or another. However, extreme insecurity is a red flag that should not be overlooked. Lack of confidence should never be a way of life or a characteristic that we accept. It most definitely shouldn't be allowed in our lives when it brings unrest and disturbance. Insecurity is then more than a flag on the play. It's a resounding whistle from the universal referee signaling you to end the game!

Another relationship killer is acting like you know it all. Sometimes you have to give up the right to be right. For some women, this task is easier said than done. However, I do know a few men that can't shut up either. I can debate with the best of them. I now realize however, that sometimes, it's okay to just be quiet. Most stains come out in the wash. The reason why this concept is so hard to grasp is because we often make mountains out of mole hills. When I look back on my marriage, I realize that sometimes we argued about dumb, insignificant things. Not only would we argue over foolishness, we would then go days without speaking to each other. I readily admit that I'm not the neatest person in the world. Hell, if you thought of five people right now, I'm probably not the neatest of any of them. I always say, "I'm clean but not neat." I wash my hands most times after using the restroom and definitely before meddling in the kitchen. However, the peanut butter is still on the counter from the sandwich I made for my daughter's lunch and although most days I make my bed, today I didn't. More often than not, my car looks as if I live in it. In my marriage, my not so neat behavior caused major arguments. Both of us felt we knew it all, but I was always determined to have the last word right before participating in an extreme moment of silence. Some things just aren't that important. Wanting to have the last word in every situation is just not that important. Going two days without speaking to your partner because you think she only drew three cards in UNO when the direction was to draw four is simply stupid. Similar occurrences happen in relationships all the time. Relationships are not always destroyed by one big event.

Sometimes they crack under the weight of a lot of petty behavior.

Communication is extremely important in relationships. Sadly, many people lay beside each other every night but still fail to communicate. When you are in a relationship with someone you are trying to build a life with, communication is indispensable. Avoiding certain topics or issues because they are uncomfortable to one or both parties is a bad idea. The scripture Luke 6:45 states that, "Out of the abundance of the heart, the mouth speaks." I take this to mean that whatever is truly within you will reveal itself in some form or fashion. Suppressed thoughts, feelings and emotions don't normally remain suppressed. It is necessary that you and your partner create a safe space within your relationship for difficult things to be discussed. Never make your partner feel like he or she can't come to you and talk in safety. No one wants to feel like it is necessary to walk on eggshells in one's own relationship. This is another life experience that I learned the hard way.

When I was married, I can remember the day we closed on our first house. I also remember the day we sold it;

moving into a townhouse with our three children. I thought my former husband and I were on the same page. I thought we both understood that selling the house opposed to allowing it to foreclose was the best thing for our family. At the time, my husband's business wasn't making enough to pay the mortgage and allow us to live comfortably. Leaving the closing and turning the keys over to the new owners, I remember expressing my sadness to him. Although I knew we were doing what was best, it didn't change the fact that I was feeling like something had just died. It felt like a huge loss. I had no idea that he took my emotions as my being disappointed in him because he didn't communicate his thoughts to me at that time. I had expressed my feelings to him because I thought it was safe. I had smiled during the closing, chatting with the new owners about how great the neighborhood was and how they were going to be so happy there. Therefore, I thought it was okay to cry on my partner's shoulder when no one was watching. However, he didn't feel it was safe for him to ask me if I was disappointed in him. Maybe he thought it would start an argument, an argument that he knew he wouldn't win because as I stated before, I liked to have the last word. Or perhaps he thought I was too weak to handle his feelings of despair. Whatever the reason, instead of communicating with me, he started another relationship with a woman outside of our marriage. When the relationship was exposed, he claimed that he simply needed someone to share his feelings with about the selling of our home. I felt completely devastated. This wasn't the first time that he had used the excuse of a lack of communication for forming outside relationships with other women. I couldn't understand it. Although I didn't always agree with him or take his words as law, I was always willing to talk, scream, yell, whatever we needed to do to express our hearts. It's also important to me to be with someone who I can share every aspect of my life. I don't want to have to be a person divided. If I can't share my hopes, dreams and fears with the same person, this isn't someone with whom I want to settle. After years of dealing with the same shit, I made the mental decision to shut him out of certain parts of my life. That was the wrong thing to do. Over time, our lack of communication ripped irreparable holes in our relationship.

Not seeing eye to eye on sexual matters can also dampen a relationship. Although I could write a whole chapter on this topic, I've decided to save it for another book. However, I'm a firm believer that contrary to what many of us are taught, sex is very important in relationships. For this reason, I'll share a few of my beliefs. First, I believe women love sex just as much as men. Secondly, when we first meet our partners, we normally make the extra effort to look nice, appealing to their physical senses. We want to look right, smell right, sound right and when the time is right, taste right. As time goes on, after we have settled into a relationship, we forget that there are other men and women that are still doing all of the above mentioned things hoping to attract a mate, maybe even yours. Therefore, I still make every effort to physically appease my mate. Although our relationship surpasses a physical or surface connection, I still take time to look good and smell good. Also, unless I'm extremely sick, I never tell him no when it comes to sex. I keep an open mind instead of constantly subjecting him to sex that's equivalent to lukewarm diarrhea in a Dixie cup. I often remind him that I'm actually hot shit in a champagne glass. In other words, keep the fires burning!

I've only been in a few serious relationships, and I've made a lot of stupid mistakes in the process. I've kissed a lot of frogs and even reproduced with them. However, what I'm most proud of is the ability to walk away from every single one of them that obviously was no good for me. Today I'm also proud to say I am the parent of three intelligent daughters. I would go through the heartache and disappointment all again if that was the only way to see their faces. I endured a lot of heartache unnecessarily. If only I had followed the advice from the "Dating 101" chapter, I may not have ended up wasting my time in fruitless relationships. Although the relationships were fun for a while and I have beautiful children as a result, they ended up going nowhere. The only way to acquire a truly successful and fruitful relationship is to enter with clear intentions and use common sense. If you lack the latter, please refer to the Chapter 6 Nuggets.

Chapter 6 Naked Nuggets:

1. GIVE UP THE RIGHT TO BE RIGHT

Pick and choose your battles. There is nothing wrong with waving a white flag if it's in the best interest of your relationship. You and your partner should be on the same team. There's no need to treat each other like enemies. The world may be a battleground but your home should always be a place of refuge.

2. COMMUNICATE, COMMUNICATE

Communication is the key. Without it, your relationship will fail. Also, always remember, it's important to talk with your partner, not at or to them. Be present when communicating, listen and make sure you understand what your partner is trying to express.

3. DON'T USE SEX OR FINANCES AS A WEAPON

Many women believe sex should be used to control their man. Both men and women use finances as a means of control. This is simply not right. Manipulation and control are weapons of mass destruction in relationships. Weapons are normally used for enemies not lovers.

4. IF THE RELATIONSHIP ISN'T WORKING, GET OUT

If for some reason you failed to enter into the relationship properly or no matter how much you've tried, it's not working, leave. I would tell you to fast, pray and put anointing oil in your partner's Kool-aid, however, that didn't work for me. Therefore my suggestion is to get out while you still can!

Chapter 7

◆◇◆

LOVE AND DIVORCE

"When shit hits the fan, learn to appreciate the brown specks on the wall."

Divorcing the man I thought I would be with for the rest of my life was the hardest thing I have ever had to do. I always thought when people got divorced it was because they hated each other. That wasn't the case for me, so I really didn't know how to handle the feeling of still loving someone that I knew wasn't good for me. Divorcing my husband was more about doing what was best for me and less about hating him for the things that had occurred in our marriage. I loved myself more than I hated him and that seemed unusual. I actually didn't hate him at all which seemed somewhat weird at the time.

Kareem and I had been together for fifteen years. We started dating when I was only twenty-two years old with a one year old daughter from a previous relationship. At the time, he had to be one of the most persistent men I had ever met. Although we had gone to high school together, we didn't run in the same circles. He was from what many call 'the wrong side of the tracks'. He grew up with roaches as pets, and I actually had a dog. He went to prison while we were still in high school for selling drugs, and it's no wonder when he approached me in a local club that I thought he was no good. However, we exchanged numbers and he would call me periodically asking to take me out and my answer was always "No!" That didn't stop him though. He would call me and beg me to call him. I never intended on giving him the time of day until he saw me walking through JC Penny's with my grandmother. I looked a hot ass mess. I had gone out that day with the thought that no one my age shopped in JC Penny's, so I probably wouldn't see anyone I knew. When he proceeded to show interest in me in front of his friend despite the fact that I looked terrible, I decided he was worth a return phone call. So I called him one night when my friends and I were headed to the movies. He invited himself to join us, but I was okay with that since we wouldn't be alone. That night we watched one of the "Faces of Death" movies. When we both laughed at the scenes that made others in the theater cringe, I decided I could definitely be more open to the possibilities of going on a real date. He vowed that he was going to see me every day even if it was only for a moment and that's exactly what he did.

We dated for four years. In hindsight, there were so many things that screamed "Neither one of you are even ready for a relationship, much less ready for marriage!" However, neither one of us listened. For starters, when we first started dating, I was still having sex with my daughter's father. Not only was I still having sex with him, I got pregnant by him for the second time. Kareem didn't walk away although he should have walked. In fact, he came by to check on me the day I had an abortion to terminate the pregnancy. Nothing changed between us and we went on with life as usual. I completely ended the relationship with my daughter's father and Kareem and I moved forward. As talkative as I am, it seemed like he talked more than I did. Kareem found his way to my house many nights just to sit and talk about his life. I was always a listening ear for him. He would sit and talk for hours as if he had never had anyone to listen to him in his life. I'm sure that the great sex, my mothering nature and ability to cook made me a good wife in his eyes. Therefore we married.

Even though the scripture states that, "It is better to marry than to burn" as mentioned earlier, the problem was that I didn't know how to be a wife and Kareem certainly didn't know how to be a husband. Neither of us grew up with role models for marriage, and we didn't understand the basic concept of not intentionally hurting someone's feelings when you love them. I was by no standards a perfect wife, but Kareem had absolutely no problem with continuously hurting my feelings year after year after year. At the time, I think the idea of being with one woman and raising children was just too much for him to handle. I also believe that his dysfunctional relationship with his mom hindered him from having the trust and vulnerability he needed to have to make our relationship work. He was used to every woman other than his grandmother betraying him. So why trust me enough to be vulnerable? This mindset was the root cause of his marital misbehavior I believe.

It's really hard to talk about my marriage in a way to help the next woman while also trying to protect my ex-husband from harsh criticism, judgment and scrutiny. Most of the time my answer to the question "Why aren't you two still together?" is this…. "I wasn't able to handle the things going on inside the home." While it's not as *naked* as some would like for me to be, it is in fact the truth. I probably would have died an early death if I had stayed and things had remained the same. Either I would've died from a stress related disease or I would have taken my own life. It is also true that Kareem could be a real asshole. During our relationship, I suffered from numerous panic attacks. It was actually too many to count. I didn't take medication, but not because it hadn't been prescribed. I had actually been on anxiety medication since the beginning of our relationship, but I didn't like the feeling the medicine gave me. If I wanted to walk around feeling like a high crack head, I would've just smoked crack. I stopped taking the medicine. However, the attacks didn't subside. They would go away for a while and then return.

Within the first year of living with Kareem and getting married, I lost about twenty pounds. Now that I think about it, my grandma tried to get me to see the red flags, alluding to the fact that the weight loss signified that there was stress in my relationship long before I said, "I do." Like so many other women, my rose colored glasses just didn't allow me to see the shit before I stepped in it. Truth is, I really wanted to be married. Perhaps I was in love with the idea of being in love. That had to be the bulk of the reason because today, I wouldn't even hold a conversation with a man who was doing the things Kareem was doing at the time, much less marry him. I knew before we walked down the aisle that he was capable of lying, cheating and calling me out of my name. I knew before we exchanged vows that there would be nights that he wouldn't come home or answer my calls. I knew I was signing up for night after night of sitting by my window waiting to recognize familiar headlights. I knew all of these things, yet I married him anyway. I saw all of these red flags but charged ahead.

I was convinced that the devil was against me, but I was stronger and would win in the end.

After saying, "I do," we went around the same bullshit circle for eleven years. I won't lie, every day wasn't a bad day. We certainly had good times or else I wouldn't have stayed so long. However, the bad times were really bad and I remember those times more vividly. Religious doctrine and the beliefs instilled in me also played a large part in my staying and trying to work things out. I can laugh about certain things now, but it was no laughing matter then. I remember in my desperation I put anointing oil in his Kool-Aid and marched around our car seven times waiting for the walls of evil to come crashing down. I swear, religion can provoke such stupidity. I found myself drowning and losing my identity. To those that knew me prior to my relationship with Kareem, I was almost unrecognizable, physically and mentally. Funny thing is that I thought God was changing me, and I was becoming a new person. The old Shemeka had passed away; all things had become new and everything new was a good thing. Therefore, all of the new foolishness I was dealing with, in my mind, was God ordained. I was willing to deal with other women, who would spell their names to me when they called to speak to my husband, if it meant I would die and hear "Well done thy good and faithful servant." When I look back at pictures from that time in my life, all I see is the walking dead. I looked older then than I do now. Under the weight of everything that was happening in my marriage, I found myself morphing into a woman that I hated. I found myself desiring another man that I may not have desired under normal circumstances. This wasn't about sex. I held on to the friendship with this man against my husband's wishes because he knew the real me and allowed me to be myself. I actually gravitated to anyone who spent more time telling me how beautiful I was or how lucky my husband was than running a list of all of my faults. I was lost and being lost contributed to the problems we faced in our marriage. In my opinion, like many men, Kareem had no problem being with other women, but the thought of his wife being with another man was unbearable.

For months, I slept in the bed with my youngest daughter. Prior to moving into her room, I slept with a butcher knife under the mattress on my side of the bed. I left only the handle out so I could access it quickly if needed. I would have dreams of Kareem killing me because I believed he hated me just that much. His actions, in my opinion, weren't the actions of a man that loved his wife. In fact, I thought I was dispensable. In the midst of all that was going on, I could not put on any weight outside of pregnancy and even then, I could never keep any of the weight after I delivered. Not only did I struggle to maintain a healthy weight, I started to lose my hair. I don't think anyone really understood that ball of fear that remained stagnate in my belly even though my face donned a smile. In the deepest part of me, I knew this relationship was no good for me, but I just couldn't leave. We had gone through so much together. He was there for me when I lost my uncle. I was there for him when his grandmother died. Before our one year wedding anniversary, he had been sentenced to prison. With the exception of two Sundays, I visited him every week with a home cooked meal. I was afraid to even try to exist without him. As a stay at home wife and mom, I had depended on him for everything, right down to my feminine products, and doubted that I could take care of myself. I felt ugly, weak and incapable of being loved.

Woman after woman, there was nothing that jolted me enough to demand more from our relationship. Finally, the biggest shift in my mindset came on a day I will never forget. I got a call from one of my close friends. She told me that she had just seen my husband riding another woman around in our truck. She even went on to describe what he was wearing. This had happened before but today was different. When I approached him about it, he became extremely defensive. I remember arguing and throwing the Kool-Aid I was drinking (there's that damn Kool-Aid again and a reason I rarely drink it now) at him before heading up the stairs to get on the computer. As I sat down at the computer, he came behind me in a rage, snatching on me and demanding that I show him what I was doing on the computer. At this point, I kicked him to get him off of me and he grabbed my leg snatching me out of the chair. As I lay helpless on the floor, he pulled back his fist and yelled at me, "I ought to beat your motherfucking ass!" My cell phone was in my back pocket, so I reached for it to call for help. I thought this might be the day that my dreams of being killed by him were going to come true. With the ugliest scowl on his face, he snatched my cell phone from me and uttered words that took me from a place that I would never return, "This is my phone. As a matter of fact everything in this house is mine!" Early in the marriage, I had dealt with years of him not coming home at night. He had even taken trips out of town only to return with his wedding ring on the opposite hand. By this time in our marriage, I had faced numerous accounts of him entertaining other women. In the past, he had called me a bitch, told me I was stupid and even said I was a dumb clown. However, these words pierced my heart unlike anything he had ever said to me before. These words revealed that he saw me as a person that was just taking up space in his life. It didn't matter to him that I had played such a pivotal role in his success. In his eyes I was nothing, had nothing and everything we had both worked so hard for belonged to him and him alone. These words and his actions that day snatched any hope that I had for our damaged relationship.

After that day, I continued to go through the motions. I pretended to be unbothered and those around me were clueless of the thoughts that ran rampant in my head on an almost daily basis. I would stand in the mirror and not recognize myself, not even the eyes looking back at me. I wanted to die because I was sure that was the only way I was going to be able to escape this horrible situation. I wrote all three of my daughters their own good-bye letter. After writing the letters, I had to figure what I was brave enough to do to end my life. What if I attempted to take my life and it didn't work, then what? These were just some of the thoughts that tormented me throughout the day home alone. I was a stay at home wife and after my husband went off to work and the kids went off to school, I would sometimes spend hours lying on the floor crying and begging God for a change. In my eyes, my husband hated me and I didn't want to live like that anymore. Many times I would spend days in bed and wouldn't eat because although I had three beautiful daughters, I felt I had no reason to live.

While there had been countless days that I wanted to die, when I found myself in the emergency room hooked up to a heart monitor, I realized I wanted more than anything to live. Perhaps this was the most severe panic attack I had ever had, or I was truly suffering from a broken heart. Whatever the case, initially the doctor in urgent care thought I could be having a real heart attack and they weren't taking any chances. After having a series of tests in the emergency room, I was fortunate enough to have a doctor who was one of the most gentle and compassionate physicians I have had. He grabbed my hand as tears streamed down my face; he went on to tell me that I couldn't continue to live the life I was living. He said it was killing me, but he said it with such kindness that I had to respect him. He didn't ask me a lot of invasive questions, and he gave me the number of some local women's groups. He also wrote me a prescription for anxiety medication. Here I was many years and two more kids later in the same predicament, needing to be on medication to cope with life. Preaching, teaching, anointed Kool-Aid, prayers, faith and speaking in tongues had only encouraged me to live a lie that was eating away at my very existence. When my husband came into the hospital room, I looked at him through tear-filled eyes and said, "If you aren't going to treat me right, please leave. This is killing me." He looked at me with such despair in his face and in a sorrowful voice said, "I'll begin to look for a place."

We all have a survival mode and it took that incident for mine to activate. Within a few weeks, I had a job. Within a few months, he moved out of our home and we've only moved forward ever since. I think it was hard for both of us initially. I responded by falling back into promiscuity briefly. I was determined to never love again. In my mind, loving someone had gotten me nowhere. Throughout the separation, Kareem remained insistent that we would reconcile. However, new rumors which many times proved true, continued to wreak havoc and eat away at any hope I had in ever trusting him again. I believe he was unsure that I would ever trust him again as well. Therefore, he would never really put himself completely out there or lay his heart on the line and for me that was a problem. We tried counseling during our separation but hearing myself speak about some things that I had never uttered out loud only pushed me closer to the decision of divorce. With all that we had endured during the marriage, I think neither of us wanted to experience anymore heartache. The final straw for me or what I call "the last lie" involved an amusement park. He had purchased more than one ticket, however his kids were home with me. I remember sitting up in my bed as tears rolled down my face. I was tired of hearing lies as well as living a lie. I was finally tired of being sick and tired. That was a Sunday morning. The next day I called the attorney and let her know that I was ready to begin the process of divorce. It happened quickly. I filed for divorce on October 12, 2012, and the divorce was final on November 26.

The day we attended court was surreal. He came to court unprepared. I think partially because he had no idea of the amazing attorney I had hired and he probably doubted my ability to stand in my strength and actually go through with it. After the judge banged the gavel, I was officially a divorced woman. Everything seemed to be moving in slow motion. I was scared because the judge had just awarded me almost eight thousand dollars a month in alimony and child support. I was afraid because I had always felt like Kareem loved money more than he loved me. None of my so called friends called to check on me that day. In fact, many of my closest friends had been fellow church members. Since I was no longer attending their church, we didn't keep in touch much. My oldest daughter had picked up her two younger sisters from school and they were waiting for me when I got there. I remember sitting with them, hugging them and feeling emotionally drained. I couldn't believe my eleven year marriage was finally over. I was relieved, but I also felt like something or someone had just died at the same time.

Fighting over money and property lasted two more years. The only property I wanted was my children's and my personal belongings, my car and my bedroom furniture. I had always promised him that I would never try to take his house and I didn't. He wanted the four bedrooms, three and a half baths to himself, so I let him have it. I just wanted to be okay and maintain somewhat of a decent lifestyle for our children. We finally settled on a monetary amount that didn't break him. Although many times I wish I wouldn't have come down on my monthly amount, it was definitely enough that wouldn't leave our children and myself hungry and homeless. I knew I had a long road of healing before me, but I was willing to do the work and move toward happiness. It was during this process of healing and strength building that I wrote the tagline that sums up my *naked* movement......

I was that chick. Gave it all up; all of it. I put all my eggs in one basket. Didn't have a plan B because I believed in plan A. Then one day it all came to an end. What was I to do? I had to take it. I'm a survivor with three kids I had to make it. So instead of dying from pain and hiding in shame, I decided to get naked!

KEEP IT NAKED

Chapter 7 Naked Nuggets:

1. GRASP REALITY

The truth was that I was now a thirty-seven year old divorced woman of three children. I had no real career because I had dedicated the majority of our marriage helping my ex-husband achieve his dreams. The relationship that I once hoped would last forever was now over and at this point, he probably hated me. To start over, a man would have to be ready to not only receive me, but also three girls. That seems like a major burden on so many different levels. Another chilling reality was that after years of praying, preaching and speaking in tongues, Jesus had not saved my marriage and I felt like I had wasted fifteen of the best years of my life. Kareem had met me when my breasts were fluffy D cups but now he was gone and I was left with two flapjacks with raisins after nursing his children.

2. FORGIVE

When I first got divorced, I wondered how I was ever going to forgive this man that I now considered an irresponsible sack of shit. First I had to identify just what I thought he had done to me and took from me. I felt like he had shattered my hopes, dreams and belief in love just to name a few things. Then I had to come to terms with the fact that he didn't own my hopes or my dreams so it wasn't in his power to restore those things. Frankly, I wasn't sure if he would, even if he could, so my best bet was to just let all of the feelings of disgust go. That allowed me to focus on all of his better attributes and really learn to appreciate him. Today my ex-husband is one of my biggest supporters and good friend.

3. CHOOSE HAPPINESS

My failed marriage was a huge disappointment for me. However, it was over and dwelling on the past only made me feel anger, bitterness and hopelessness. After separating and then divorcing, I dated a man who was younger than me. Though it didn't work, I decided to take a chance on love with him and I was proud of that. After all, it didn't sound as crazy as sitting around waiting for karma to strike my ex-husband. I just wanted to live in the moment. I finally settled down with a great man. Choosing happiness day to day has continued to be a central focus.

4. LIVE

This has to be the four letter word that is most overlooked. When it's all said and done, no matter what we go through in life, we can do nothing else if we don't first LIVE!

Chapter 8

◆◇◆

FINANCES

"Money is the solution to all bills!"

My credit is fucked! As stated in the previous chapter "Love and Divorce" I was a stay at home wife. However, as much as I would like to blame someone else, I can't blame anyone but myself. It was me that put my future in someone else's hands. It was me that allowed someone else to play with my credit. The best advice I can give someone when it comes down to finances is "Protect yourself!" When I met my ex-husband, my credit score was in the 700s. While that's not impeccable credit, it's still considered pretty good. I had worked for the State Employees' Credit Union and prior to working there I was required to pay off any outstanding debts. They didn't want employees to be tempted in any way to do something immoral. Therefore moving forward with no debt, a full-time job and a car loan that was automatically drafted from my account, I was in good standing financially. I was doing extremely well but then came love and dumb decisions.

Initially, I didn't see my decisions as stupidity. I saw them as choices that would put our family ahead. Once I said, "I do" I did, for better or worse. Somehow though, it seems like the decisions we made for our family worked out for his "better" and were always worse for my credit. I don't think at that time anyone could have told me anything different because I was in love. I was sure that every financial decision I made was going to work out great in the end because I was being selfless and putting my family first. The truth is that was a loaded crock of crap! Yes, I was in love. Yes, I was making decisions to put my family in a better place, but I was doing all of this to my personal detriment. In hindsight, which is always twenty-twenty, our financial status as a married couple would have been much stronger with both of us in great financial standing. However, with one child and another one on the way, I was about to be a stay at home mom and this is when I began to undervalue myself financially. My last tax refund as a working individual was six thousand dollars. At the time, I had a few unpaid medical bills and a couple of bills from insurance agencies. We would decide the bill was too high, jump ship and leave it unpaid, which was always solely in my name. I should've taken some of that tax refund and paid off my outstanding debts. At this point in my life, I can't even understand what frame of mind I must have been in to totally ignore my own needs. However, it was our desire to buy a house and I wasn't working. Therefore, the decision was made to take my six thousand dollars in tax refunds and apply it to my husband's debt. After all, he was going to be the only name on the mortgage as he was the only one bringing in any income. When Kareem got home from prison, he said God told him to start his own company. With the knowledge I had gained by working in corporate America, I did everything I could to help him. I found a logo, created a business résumé and typed up a general contract. Prior to our relationship, Kareem didn't know how to write a check. However, I never looked at him as unintelligent. He definitely knew how to make money. Therefore, I believed with his ambition, business sense (although illegal) and the knowledge I had acquired from years of working, we would make a great team. There was no doubt in my mind that his business would be successful. Therefore, the decisions we made concerning finances, made perfect sense to me then. We also made the agreement that after we paid off his debt, we would pay off the debt we had created in my name. This would be done once we were in our own home and more established. Of course, that never happened. I would be remiss not to point out the fact that Kareem worked extremely hard to provide for our family. If it wasn't for the huge ego that controlled his behavior, I could have sung his praises.

I continued to be a fool in love. We continued to use my name for all of the bullshit bills that we knew wouldn't directly affect us. When our kids went to the doctor, I always signed the dotted line as the party responsible for the bill. Together we looked as if we were sitting on top of the world. We had a beautiful home with at least two luxury cars in the driveway. If we would've had our own reality television show, it could have been called "Keeping up with the Carpenters." However structurally, our finances were a joke. I remember being completely frustrated at one point that we had two Mercedes Benzes, but no health insurance or college fund for our children. On an individual level, my husband was thriving. He had a growing business with a house and cars in his name. For the most part, he paid these large bills on time. Therefore over the years, his credit score improved. Although I was an authorized user on his credit cards which helped my credit score, wearing rose colored glasses for so many years, really hurt my finances. Once we divorced, I was ass out! I had worked a full time job for only a little over a year. All of our major purchases had been in his name only, and I had a string of petty debt that was now looking me right in the face. For this reason, once I left the marital home, I had a hard time finding a place for my children and I to live. Not only was I a credit risk, my ex-husband initially refused to follow the court orders as outlined. That left me looking like I had limited steady income and no control over my own finances. After years of playing "Duck, Duck Goose" with my finances, shit had just got real!

Many times women are taught to wait for a man to make major life decisions. Prior to this relationship, I wanted to buy a town home but my mother talked me out of it. She said that I would eventually get married and buy a house with my husband. It sounded like a better plan than buying a house alone, and my mom was right. I did in fact get married and bought a house with my husband, but I was only a tenant. If I had purchased my own townhouse prior to marriage, not only would I have had income while I was a stay at home mom, I would've had a place to go back to once the shit hit the fan. I also wouldn't be preparing to move for a third time in four years. My plea to you is simply, "Don't be stupid!" Setting yourself up for financial success does not mean that you don't believe your relationship will work. Preparing for a "just in case" doesn't necessarily mean that you are betting against your happily ever after either. Think of it this way, it is better for both parties to be in a great place financially and anyone that cares about you will want you to be able to function without them. This isn't just in the case of divorce. This will also protect you in the event of disability or the death of your spouse.

Now that I have three daughters, I can use my own life experiences to teach them how to be financially responsible and be in love. My oldest daughter has traveled abroad to both Greece and Italy. She along with her two younger sisters have recently started their own business. Although my ex-husband may never admit how stupid I was, I definitely believe that he would never want his daughters to make the same choices. He is very adamant about them being successful and being able to stand on their own. I've never heard him teach them that they need to wait on a man to come along to validate them or create success for them. My life lessons have been beneficial in teaching both of us how to teach our daughters.

Another thing I've learned in life when it comes to finances is to say no. I've put myself in situation after situation just by being too nice or too helpful. People will judge you based on what they think they see or understand about your finances. If they feel you are better off than they are, some of them will seek you out and try to use you for their benefit. Always trying to help someone out is another mistake, a mistake that can leave you in the bathroom stall after a bowel movement with no tissue. Remember this saying, "Never let anyone borrow what you can't afford to let them have!"

Chapter 8 Naked Nuggets:

1. WORRY ABOUT YOURSELF

There is nothing wrong with being in a relationship and working as a team. However, never do this to the detriment of your well-being. Sure your relationship may last 'til death do you part, but according to Proverbs 22:1, "A good name is rather to be chosen than riches and gold." A partner that truly cares about you will want you to be equally successful. A caring partner will never put you in a position where you can barely stand on your own. However, ultimately, it is up to you to protect and guard your best interests. Your finances and your financial portfolio are your responsibility.

2. DON'T BE BLINDED BY LOVE

Love is a splendid thing but we really can make some dumb ass decisions when we let it blind us. Loving someone doesn't mean you have to be a pushover or run into oncoming traffic. Love should never be the reason to make any decision that is not in your best interest. Loving others should never come at the expense of loving yourself, point blank period!

3. YOUR FUTURE WILL ONE DAY BE YOUR PRESENT

Many times we make dumb decisions because we are only thinking about right now. We fail to realize that our future will one day be our present and the decisions that we make right now will have a major effect on our future. Although you may not be psychic, it's important to predict and plan for your future. While it's important to enjoy life and be grateful for what is, certain preparation should be made for what's to come. Poor financial decision making can have a huge impact on your future and based on our economic system, there is really no way around that.

Chapter 9

♦◇♦

PARENTING

"The best job that you sometimes want to quit but shouldn't."

Sometimes I wish people had to get licensed to become parents. Then again, considering I had my first child before I was completely ready to provide the best lifestyle for her, my license would've probably been denied. Also, considering I'm a black female, we would've received licenses well after most other races and only after some marches, walk outs or sit-ins. However, some people definitely don't deserve kids. I get so upset when I see a mom screaming and cursing at her child as if he or she asked to be brought into the world. Some parents act like children are such a burden. Yet many of them are the same parents that continue to have child after child.

Of course, there's no manual on how to be a good parent. Yet I believe that when the love is there, you do what you need to do to figure it out. I'm sure love is what made my mom such an attentive and great parent. She was always there, yelling my name the loudest. Of all my recitals, band performances, award days, parent/teacher conferences, etc, I only remember her missing one important event. That was junior prom and it was only because she had a nursing conference that she had to attend. She has been and still is one of my greatest supporters. Will you make mistakes as parents along the way? Of course! My youngest daughter once told me that having my oldest daughter was just practice and I obviously messed up a little bit. I couldn't agree with her more. I definitely coddled her for way too long creating a young adult that isn't as independent as she could be. I completely doted over her and every aspect of her life. I learned as a parent to my oldest daughter, that I need to stop being such a helicopter mom who is always hovering. It's so easy to slide into the role of trying to fix everything, but it only handicaps the child. Some people believe children are sent here for us to control and attempt to make them into our little mini me's. Even if you know you are full of it and one person like you is enough for the world, many of us still set out to make our kids just like us. The woman who has been left by a man to raise her kids on her own, often times raises her son to be just like the man that left her. If she has daughters, she continues to exemplify behavior that will only lead her daughters to attract the same kind of man. Fathers often encourage their children to be just like them as well. Often times this leads to adults incapable of having stable relationships. No one really prepares parents or equips us with the knowledge that we are rearing little people. Children are not here for us to rule or control. I learned this the hard way after my oldest daughter at nineteen, came to me with the fact that she was attracted to girls. Everything I had ever imagined for her seemed to crumble in an instant. I thought, "Damn it, I need to fix this!" I immediately started trying to figure out where I went wrong. Was she angry at men because her biological dad had been an absent parent or was she upset with her stepdad for the bullshit she witnessed from him? Did she look at me and think I was a spineless wimp of a woman who allowed men to control me, so she vowed to be nothing like me? I became sad thinking that I would never help her plan her wedding. I wondered if she was going to want to start dressing more masculine or cut her beautiful hair. I obsessed over what others would think about her or even what they would think about me and my parenting skills. Then I pictured her kissing a girl and I almost vomited in my mouth. "What did I do to deserve this?" I thought. I must have been too liberal. Suddenly living *naked* seemed like a bad idea. The whole concept was backfiring! It took a while for me to understand that I was actually being an example, allowing her to remove her mask and live freely. Then I had to grab and shake myself because her being bisexual or gay, whatever she chose, really wasn't that serious. When I really thought about it, she was the same young lady that I absolutely adored, regardless of the gender with whom she decided to live life. At the end of the day, it's her life and I want her to live it to its fullness. As long as she was not harming herself or anyone else, there was nothing for me to try and rationalize or fix. I honestly still don't like her choices in partners but even with that, I only offer a listening ear when she needs it and I try my best to refrain from any "I told you so" statements. I salute my beautiful daughter for living life authentically.

Sometimes we expect our children to be perfect but fail to realize that we are not perfect in our role as parents. More often than not, I have a pile of unfolded clothes that need to be put away. Then there's another load that sits in the dryer because I don't have time to fold it and I don't want to add to the pile that's already been sitting for days. There are days that I'm so exhausted from running behind my two younger ones that I can barely breathe (I'm probably just out of shape though). Add to that a college student with young adult issues and I feel like my work is never done. Sometimes I don't even feel like being creative for dinner. I want to serve the same old quick meal and after a long day, have *them* tuck *me* into bed. Sometimes, I feel like I truly suck at parenting! Thankfully though there's no big hand that reaches out of nowhere to slap the shit out of me for being a total fuck up. I try to show my children that same grace. Although I don't completely disagree with corporal punishment, I also don't believe in beating children for every little thing. Again, children are little people. If you believe in reincarnation, they are little people that have been here before. I totally believe our children are here to teach us something about ourselves. Sometimes the things we need to learn aren't so nice or don't show us in our best light. I ended up with all girls and sometimes I wonder if the gods were playing some sort of cruel joke on me. While I love these girls more than I could ever explain, sometimes they irritate the hell out of me. Sometimes they get attitudes, walk away from me while I'm talking, talk back to me and fail to use good judgment. While I'm still figuring out exactly what this is supposed to teach me, I've certainly had to learn and exercise a great deal of patience. Sometimes, I've blatantly failed at this endeavor. However, as I watch parents completely go off on their children for what appears to be no reason, I'm learning to count to ten. I have to constantly remind myself that they are little people. Sometimes worry and or disappointment causes them to misbehave or act in an inappropriate way just as those things affect adults. Beating them into oblivion solves nothing. It doesn't even make most parents feel good.

Parenting is simpler than we make it. Our greatest responsibility is to provide an environment for our children to thrive.

SINGLE PARENTING

As stated in chapter 5, my first daughter was by a married man. Although I entered into a serious relationship when she was a year old, we didn't start living together until she was four and even then, my mate didn't immediately take on the father role. He was more like a cool uncle. So, I was left for the first few years of her life to raise her alone. In fact, like me, many women have had to raise kids alone because we made poor choices, spreading our legs to the wrong men. If you are raising a child alone and the other parent didn't die, more than likely you chose the wrong person as a co-parent. Even if you never marry, a good man or woman will never leave you to be a single parent. The only blame in this situation is poor decision making. Effective parenting starts well before conception with choosing a partner that will be a good parent. My ex-husband often says he purposely waited to have children until he knew they would have a good mom. More often than not, people are lying down with partners they don't even like, much less a person who is a good fit as a parent. If you can't even make wise decisions about whom you have sex with, in my opinion, you definitely aren't ready to be a responsible parent. Many of us plow ahead anyway. However, instead of using the fact that I had a child that I had to take care of without the help of the father as an excuse, having my first daughter was actually my biggest motivation to succeed. My mom had always said to me "Mama's baby, daddy's maybe." Therefore, I knew as a single mom, I was going to be responsible for holding down the fort. I always knew that I wanted my daughter to have a good life even when it didn't look like I had the means to provide it. To this day, I'm determined to be a positive example to her and her two younger siblings.

After having my daughter at twenty-one years old, I had to grow up real quick. Sometimes, she says that she doesn't want any children simply because of all the sacrifices she's watched me make over the years. However, they are all sacrifices that I wouldn't change. Growing up didn't happen overnight though. Having the abortion that I spoke of in Chapter 5 was my first big girl parenting decision. I was a little girl who decided to spread her legs once again to a man that had already shown me that he wasn't capable of being an involved father on which either of us could depend. So although I had always been a pro-life advocate, I made the very tough decision to terminate the pregnancy knowing that I could not efficiently take care of two children. I also knew that I didn't want to live in public housing dependent on government assistance. To the disagreement of many, that abortion was one of the best parenting decisions I have ever made. In my opinion, good or bad parenting starts before conception. I had no business conceiving a second child under those circumstances. That was a bad parenting choice, but I was determined to make it right and not make the same mistake again and I didn't. Some would say I took the easy way out and I should've been responsible from the beginning. Of course, they're right. But the truth was, I had been irresponsible and that was the only decision that seemed right to me at the time.

CO-PARENTING

When I divorced, I felt like a complete failure. More than failing myself I felt like I had failed my three children. I had failed them not only because I wasn't able to hold our family together, but also because now I was contributing to them being raised in a broken home just as I had been raised. That was never my wish for my three beautiful daughters.

What hurts me the most is the pain it has caused my oldest daughter. She made the statement over dinner that she didn't have a dad. At first I was slightly confused. I wasn't questioning her statement as it pertained to her biological dad because he hadn't been consistently present. However, I needed to know why she felt this way about the man who had been in her life since she was a year old. Still confused and apparently naïve to her true feelings, I explained to her that my ex-husband still considered her to be his daughter. She politely said that because we were no longer married that technically he was no longer her stepdad. Not considering her feelings, I continued to press the issue that marriage or shall I say divorce didn't matter. I was totally oblivious to the fact that our divorce may have had a negative effect on her. Therefore, I thoughtlessly continued to talk. That's when she finally looked at me and said sternly "Outside of buying us things, he doesn't act like a daddy and he doesn't treat me like a daughter!"

That's the moment my heart broke and those initial feelings of failure began to creep in again. Not only had I failed her once but twice. Not only had she experienced rejection from her biological father because I made the wrong choice, but now she was feeling rejection by the only man she had called dad. Words cannot express the flood of emotions I felt as I continued to eat and try to pretend like nothing was wrong. I cried quietly in the shower. I cried silently as he called each of his biological children to speak with them but her phone never rang.

I'm sure there were times that she gave him attitude and maybe he felt like he shouldn't have to take that. However, she's a teenager. Some days she gives me attitude and I'm sure there are millions of other parents who have experienced this with their teenager. For me, there is nothing she or any of my children could do that would change the way I feel about them. As Netty cried out in the Color Purple "Only death could keep me from it." I would never walk away, abandon, cut off, forget about, ignore, disown or divorce my child. Maybe he was clueless to her feelings just as I was.

I'm struggling and wondering how this is going to affect her adult life. Will she hate men? Will she go out of her way to get or hold their attention? This is hurting me so badly; I can hardly gather my thoughts. Every parent wants to fix whatever is wrong in their child's life, but I feel this is out of my control. I have never been that baby mama that tries to keep the children away from the father. I could partially understand if that was the case but it's not. My/our daughter is so beautiful inside and out and I'm having the hardest time understanding why any parent wouldn't move heaven and earth to be there for her and be proud to say and show they're her parent.

All hell broke loose when I posted that blog a few years ago. Perhaps my ex-husband was initially embarrassed by the fact that his life wasn't in fact as perfect as he portrayed it to be. I couldn't understand why someone would be so vindictive, caring more about gossip about him than a hurting teenager. Before he even took the time to read the blog, his bruised ego had prompted him to call me on the telephone to give me a piece of his mind, that in my opinion, he needed every bit. I have never set out to drag his reputation through the mud, but he is in fact a part of my story and my truth. Although he was yelling at me over the phone, coming through louder than the fans at the basketball game I was attending, I didn't regret releasing the story because it produced positive results. We decided that it would be best if he, our daughter and I sat down and talked. Although our relationship had failed, like it or not, he held a special place in our daughter's heart. I had a sincere interest to see their relationship succeed because it was in her best interest. We wanted to give our daughter an opportunity to express her feelings. I felt like he needed to understand that I only wrote how I felt as a result of how she was feeling. Prior to the meeting, she made me promise not to cry. However, it was she that shed tears as she painted a picture that was too bold and vivid for either one of us to ignore. Listening to her allowed us to see just how this divorce was affecting the people we loved the most. Our children had made no decision to be in this position, yet they were just as affected as he and I were if not more so. Remember, the children are the top priority. Many times after couples split, they get caught up in winning or trying to prove a point to the other person. They forget they share what is most important…the child. Your main concern as a parent should be to stabilize your children by any means necessary. Being the best parent possible requires you to set aside bruised egos and foolish pride. Whether you know it or not, children can sense when mom and dad are at odds. Many times it causes a sense of unrest within the children as they feel pressure to choose a side. This should never be a child's concern. The child's well-being should always outweigh any asinine pettiness.

This was one of many conversations that my ex-husband and I would have as we figured out how to co-parent. One thing we were sure of was that we loved our girls very much and only wanted the best for them. Because neither parent is given a manual, it's important to support one another when parenting gets difficult. When you notice or sense that your co-parent is feeling inadequate, offer encouragement. If you notice areas that need improvement for the sake of the children, be willing to discuss those things rationally. In addition to talking, be willing to listen. Not once did I think that being a good listener meant that we would see eye to eye on every situation, but I was confident that we would work together to figure things out for the sake of our children. Parenting has been one of my greatest joys. Kaylah believes that I am understanding and open minded. Kylah and Kelyse tell me all the time that I am a great mother. These are wonderful compliments to receive from your children. I'm also appreciative that my ex-husband thinks I'm capable, trusts me and supports me in being a great mom.

Chapter 9 Naked Nuggets:

1. IN CO-PARENTING, GET OVER EACH OTHER

This seems like a no brainer. However, just because couples split, it doesn't mean they are completely over one another. Many times constant bickering is due to unresolved emotional baggage. When one or both parents are unforgiving or holding feelings of resentment, it can have a tremendous effect on the person's ability to let go and move forward. If the relationship was abusive in any way, it's important that you deal with your co-parent under new standards. Continuing abusive behavior will hinder your co-parenting efforts. However, if you find yourself constantly getting angry with your co-parent and using your child as a pawn, ask yourself "Am I really over him/her?"

2. REMEMBER, CHILDREN ARE LITTLE PEOPLE

Children are little people that will one day grow up to be big people. How functional they are as adults will greatly depend on how well they were reared as children. Look at how you are raising your children and ask yourself this question, "Am I raising someone that will be an asset to society or a total fuck up?"

3. PROVIDE AN ENVIRONMENT FOR YOUR CHILDREN TO THRIVE

As a former school employee, I have seen so many things that left me wondering why certain people even chose to reproduce. Some people seem to only have children for bigger tax refunds. Raising children is a big responsibility and providing an environment for them to thrive in every area of life, should be taken seriously. If you can't or refuse to meet this basic qualification, consider abstinence or birth control!

Chapter 10

◆◇◆

FRIENDSHIP

"Many people may jump on your boat but only real friends will help you row."

I don't like needy ass women. If we don't share DNA, I don't want to have to talk to any woman every day all day. I don't want to have long drawn out crying sessions over the nature of our friendship. Also, I don't want our relationship to be emotionally charged and I'm too old for regular sleepovers. In my opinion, there are a lot of women that aren't looking for friends. Some of their bestie behavior borders lesbianism. They are too jealous and needy. Most grown women that have partners and/or children and jobs, don't have time for that. Then there are some that believe that friendship is overrated. Therefore, they fail to make connections with anyone although they long for a genuine friendship. I'm somewhere in the middle. Sometimes we just fail to understand what a friend really is and put unrealistic expectations on the wrong people.

After "blogging" on Facebook and sharing a very personal experience, I asked my friends not to let the people crucify me as I became the first "Naked Girlz" hence, the name and concept was born. "It's about to be more ex-Naked Girlz than Naked Girlz." That statement made by an old friend makes me laugh. Depending on how well you know me or how closely you follow my blog, you may have noticed that in the beginning things were different. Initially, the original "Naked Girlz" bloggers were my close friends. Before "Naked Girlz" began, my friends and I discussed my desire to have a blog. I shared that recent life events had left me feeling alone and misunderstood. Since I have kept a personal journal since 1997, I thought a blog would allow me to share my life with others. I also knew many of their personal stories, so I felt they had a lot to offer as well. However, I wasn't looking for just another Facebook. I didn't want just a bunch of surface level, sugarcoated writings. I also didn't want a depressing site, but rather a good mix of real, heart grabbing topics plus some light hearted fun material. They all thought the blog was a great idea.

Because it was my idea, I didn't think it was fair to ask my friends for money especially since they would be investing their time. Over the next few months, I went to work setting up and branding my business. It quickly became clear however that drawing the line between friendship and business would be more difficult than I thought. Unfortunately, my desire to include my friends outweighed my inner voice and several outer voices that kept telling me it was a bad idea. In my opinion, the disrespect began when it started to appear that my friends didn't take my vision seriously. Late or missed blogs came with excuses such as "I had a headache," "I didn't have anything to talk about" or simply, "I forgot." This was my vision, so I continued to write, exposing my deepest feelings and staying true to the brand. Suddenly, instead of receiving blogs, I began to receive resignation letters. In the letters, I was criticized for my writing style and being too open. I was irritated to say the least because my vision had always been clear, and the name itself signified my purpose of being honest and open. My vision was my baby and to flippantly mishandle it was a blatant slap in my face. Twenty years of friendship dissolved, and initially, I was angry. Then I took time to look at the situation and ask myself where I went wrong.

What changed? I had grown up but had held on to my childhood view of our friendship. We were a group of women who had a tight knit friendship when we were younger. However in adulthood, we rarely, if ever, supported one another. Births, deaths, marriages and divorces all went unsupported. Though I knew we loved each other, I was in denial about what that love meant. I was thinking because they loved me, they would grab hold of my vision, run with it and protect it. Then we would celebrate over wine as we watched it blossom. After all, that's what happened when we decided to participate in a step competition in high school. We worked together day after day until we came together to completely embarrass the other team on our school's tennis courts. But we hadn't had that type of friendship in years. Our friendship was now limited to coming together every couple of years to have dinner and post a few pictures. I was living in the past; I think we all were living in the past. We had been estranged for years, and there was nothing connecting us that would allow them to understand why I was so passionate about this endeavor.

I've learned that as we mature, things change. The roles that friends play in our lives also change. Early in life, we share affinities such as nice clothes. We make friends according to the neighborhood we grow up in or shared interests in extracurricular activities. However, what happens when we grow up and no longer live in the same neighborhood? What do we do when we are raising our families and don't need to borrow each other's clothes? We adjust to life's changes, understanding that many times our friendships will be limited to occasional gatherings and support. And for me, when there's no support combined with an effort to tear me down, there's no reason to portray a fake friendship. While the love will always continue, like in other areas of my life, I have to create and uphold boundaries even in friendships. When I truly care for

161

someone, I really try to see the good in him or her. But I've realized that this can be done from afar. It's important that we place the people in our lives in the respective categories in which they belong. Don't have unrealistic expectations. Expect them to be who they've shown you they are; this will limit disappointment. When I realized that I had friends that weren't going to support what I was doing, I had to suck it up like a big girl and move forward. I don't believe their lack of support was from a place of hatred. Living *naked* just wasn't a shared interest. I had to learn to be okay with that. I had to trust that the universe would bring into my life what I envisioned: other women tired of wearing masks. I was sick of phony friendships and wanted more. I wanted a friend that believed in me just as much as I believed in myself. I wanted a friend that would support me in any way possible. Even if we rarely talked, my friend's support would be seen and felt consistently. I had to have this type of friend because that's the type of friend I am. Although time doesn't permit me to sit and chat on the phone with my friends every day for hours, when it counts, I'm there.

I've realized that as I've decided to live *naked* and authentic, everything that isn't real is fading and I'm attracting what I need at this time in my life. Now, my closest friends are those that see me as the woman I am today and believe in where I want to go. Sometimes it's hard to let go of who or what you are familiar with, especially friends. I've learned that as you shift and grow in life, the people that occupy your personal universe may shift as well. It's important that you don't hold on to any relationship just for the sake of having it. Amongst your true friends, you should never have to make apologies for who you are. Real friends never require you to shrink or downplay who you are for their comfort. They celebrate you in all that you are and desire for you to achieve every positive goal you set out to achieve.

Chapter 10 Naked Nuggets:

1. DETERMINE IF THEY ARE FRIENDS OR SIMPLY FAMILIAR

Friends may change over the years. As we grow, if our relationships don't adjust with us, there may be a need to make some changes. It's okay to leave familiar relationships in the past and form new bonds with people who have your best interest at heart.

2. DON'T HAVE UNREALISTIC EXPECTATIONS

Sometimes we set ourselves up for disappointment. We look to people to be who we wish they were or who they used to be. When they fail to meet those expectations, many of us become angry or hurt. We also look to outside sources for what we should possess inwardly. Don't be a needy friend. Never look to another to make you happy or bring joy. That's too much responsibility to put on another human being.

3. BE A FRIEND, TO HAVE A FRIEND

In order to have real connections even in friendship, imagine yourself in the other person's shoes. In no relationship is it wise to be unbalanced. Every relationship, including platonic friendships, must have equal give and take.

Chapter 11

◆◇◆

CAREER

If you don't work on your dreams, someone will hire you to work on theirs   ~Unknown~

From the strip club to the pulpit to living by the beat of my own drum, I did it all *naked*, blunt and straight to the point. Unless I'm angry, I speak with all sincerity even if the truth stings. But how could I make a career from that? Wasn't that just simply my personality? Is what Gary Zukav said true? Should your personality rise up to meet your purpose? And if that was true, could I make a career from living my purpose? I had worked on someone else's dreams for many years. Now I really wanted to work on mine! With all of these things in mind and believing that my purpose could lead me to the career I desired, I decided to do everything *naked*. Initially my vision for Naked Girlz was to provide a community of people that would be honest and could identify with the lives of others. I was so sick of people sitting in shit puddles pretending like they didn't smell anything. So many of us have beat the odds and overcome extremes such as domestic violence, rejection, abandonment, rape, child molestation, homelessness and infidelity just to name a few. In this community, we would cover real topics, share real feelings and provoking thoughts about real issues. I wanted to have *naked* conversations about issues that people face every day but are uncomfortable discussing. I believed in that vision even if I stood by myself. The bottom line is that sometimes you must go alone. I couldn't let my vision die, so I chose to believe in myself and stayed focused.

From the initial excitement of the *Naked Girlz Blog* and many hopping on board, to all of the initial writers and supporters calling it quits, I had to keep going. Once I started, there was no looking back and a few fair-weathered friends weren't going to change that. After a year of blogging, I resigned from my full time job. Not because it didn't pay well or have excellent benefits. The pay was decent and the benefits were great and certainly needed by my family and I. However, it didn't line up with my passion, so I decided to walk away. I knew many people would stare at me like deer caught in headlights. For some, the concept of following your passion or finding your personal legend has yet to become a reality for them and that's quite okay. Next to filing for divorce, leaving my job was one of the hardest decisions I knew I had to make. I knew there was something more for me than budgets and bloody noses.

The mixed reactions from people were quite interesting to watch. People that are driven solely by money saw my job as financial security and couldn't understand why I would walk away from it. All of their questions were and still are about finances. They asked questions such as "How will you support yourself?" or "When will you go back to work?" They didn't understand that I felt like my true career should be tied to my purpose. Many of them stated they could not or would not leave their job, and some of them would say it with a "You are stupid" undertone. Then there were those that admired my courage and applauded the strength it took to step out on faith into the unknown. So many people began to share their passions with me, and I found myself doing exactly what I set out to do, facilitate freedom.

Was I scared? I was a little afraid. There was definitely some initial fear of the unknown, but in fact, handing in my resignation was my first step of overcoming the fear of failing. Also, I had assisted my ex-husband in building a business that grossed almost half a million dollars per year. I had seen it done and believed I was able to do it for myself. I was so excited to get busy! I was thrilled about having the opportunity to share the victories of my life experiences. I looked forward to living life authentically, on purpose with purpose, and watching others do the same.

Of course I realize not everyone can just quit their job to pursue their passion. However, everyone can take a step in that direction. I understand that some people will say they aren't sure of their purpose. Honestly, I feel like I wasted the first year after coming out of work just trying to figure out the direction in which I should be moving. I can attest the more you get to know yourself and stand in your truth, the more apparent your purpose becomes. The more you follow that purpose, a career and way to monetize it will arise. Each and every one of us has the power to acquire wealth. Happiness comes from within. For me, happiness is being successful and real success is living your purpose in a career that you love. I knew I wanted to write a book, but until the last few months, my much anticipated book was just words on a paper with no direction. My main focus is helping people. I knew that my purpose and career would go hand in hand because that's what I desired. As I live my purpose, every job I decide to do must line up with that. Whether I'm writing, speaking or offering personal empowerment, it goes hand in hand with living *naked*, strong and free!

Until this all began, I had no idea that the word *naked* would be offensive to so many people. I got a lot of backlash from outsiders (and insiders too to be truthful) due to my use of the word. At first I couldn't understand the big deal. Why did the word *naked* make so many people uncomfortable? I've since made the determination that it's not so much the word but the act itself. We have gotten so comfortable with being fake, that the thought of opening up and allowing the world to see our imperfections seems absolutely absurd. I could easily write and speak about ingrown toenails. I'm sure someone somewhere could identify with the pain, especially when your sock is too tight or someone accidentally steps on your foot. However, I'd rather reach that man or woman who is feeling the weight of the world on his or her shoulders and ready to drive the car and kids into a lake. I want her to know she's not alone. I'd rather reach that man prior to him jumping from a bridge or from the deck of a parking garage. I believe that if you've overcome something, it is best to share it to help someone else overcome it. If you've conquered what you thought was unconquerable, pay it forward and tell someone how to have the same victory.

I realize what this costs. I realize that people will make judgments about who I am based on the things that make me angry, happy or scared. I realize that some people are so comfortable pretending to be perfect that revealing my imperfections may make them uncomfortable. I realize that it may be difficult for people to undress with me exposing their own flaws all for the sake of helping others. But I'm on a mission to start a *naked* movement. That's my purpose,

and from that purpose I'm going to make a career!

Chapter 11 Naked Nuggets:

1. LOOK AT YOUR LIFE

Look at your life and be honest with yourself. If you hate the career you've chosen, admit that. Determine exactly what it is that you hate about it. It could be as simple as you love your job, but you wish you were making more money. If that's the case, don't be afraid to look for something else. Remember if you always do what you've always done, you'll always get what you've always gotten. However, if you are completely miserable and you know you chose that career for all of the wrong reasons, don't waste the rest of your life being miserable. Sure you may not be able to suddenly quit your job, but there are small things that you can do towards your ultimate goal.

2. IGNORE THE NAYSAYERS

You are the creator of your own life. Don't let it be governed by simple simpletons. Perhaps others were too afraid to go after what they really wanted in life, but that doesn't mean you should be afraid. What's your purpose? How can you monetize that and make it into a career? "Life is short" is a popular phrase. However life is long as hell when you're spending most of it dissatisfied. Block out the negative opinions of others and go after what you want.

3. DON'T LOOK BACK

Once you make the decision to go after what you want in life, you may have days of doubt. I certainly did, especially after a year of staring at a word count that would not go above one thousand. However, there will always be joy in knowing that even in your doubt, you are doing what so many others dream of doing but are afraid to do.

Chapter 12

◆◇◆

LIVE LIFE AUTHENTICALLY

"To live life authentically, to me, is the only way to live."

We get so caught up in what others think about our lives that sometimes we forget to live. As a former ordained minister, I'm sure there are several congregations of people that look at me now and can't believe their eyes. I'm sure I have been the talk of many conversations or even an example of a backslider. I'm sure the ones that think their prayers pave the way to heaven have rolled in the floor with tears streaming down their faces, speaking in tongues and calling my name. How dare I want to live a life of honesty: good, bad or indifferent? How dare I desire to take off the masks that I've worn for years? The nerve of me to want to be happy. The nerve of me to want to be open about my real life experiences. The nerve of me to want to set out on a mission to be free and encourage others to do the same. Call in the troops; it is time to fast and pray!

Some people will even try and disassociate themselves from the foolishness above by saying, "I don't have a problem with what she's doing. I just think she could be doing it differently. You know, with less curse words and refraining from talking about enjoying sex." Basically what they are saying is, "I don't like how free she is because I live such a restricted lifestyle. Her openness makes me uncomfortable." All of that is insecure bullshit from unhappy people.

I will sit and talk to Oprah Winfrey...only death can keep me from it! If we can believe in Santa Claus, the Easter bunny and the tooth fairy for the first eight to ten years of our lives, why can't we believe in ourselves? Many believe in a Savior we have only read about but doubt ourselves when we can see, feel and move in our own being every day. We have been conditioned to look outside of ourselves for everything when everything we need is already within us.

Do you know how great you are? Do you know that there is no one like you on this planet? So, why do most people wait for validation from outside sources to believe how special they are? Don't get me wrong, I appreciate outside appreciation. Without it, this book would have been a waste of my time. I wouldn't have sat down to write it though if I didn't believe in myself first. I appreciate and have learned from every experience I've had in life, and I truly believe that gives me something to offer the world. The knowledge of self gave me the guts to start a blog, begin vlogging, speak publicly and write a book. Sometimes you must have an "I don't give a fuck" attitude. If you focus on the opinions of people, you may never get anywhere. I truly believe that there are a lot of people that don't realize how stupid they are anyway. Why base my life around whether they accept me or not? Why should you base your whole life around the acceptance of stupid people?

I've been asked what gave me the courage to want to live *naked*. My answer is that after my divorce, I felt like I had nothing left to lose. Imagine walking away from a beautiful home, security and everything on which you had based your future. Imagine losing friends. Most of them stopped talking to me during my divorce because they felt compelled to choose a side and didn't know which side to take. To solve the problem created in their tiny minds, they just stopped talking to me altogether. Therefore, I was left to face one of my most difficult life experiences without some of the people that had claimed to love me unconditionally. In my eyes, I had lost almost everything. What else was left to lose? I knew my kids would love me no matter what. My mom had already proven that she was going to stand by me no matter what, so anyone outside of those four people didn't matter a damn.

From the day a heartless stranger forcibly released life into my mother alone in the woods. To the day I stared in the mirror as a child crying because I was black with big lips and nappy hair. The day I held a gun to another woman's head. The day I removed all of my clothes gyrating in a room full of men for money. The day I was robbed at gunpoint. The day I gave birth to my first daughter without her father. The day I stood at the pulpit saying, "I do" believing my life had just begun. The day I stood in the pulpit proclaiming what I believed to be the word of God. The day I was devastated by news of "the other" woman. The day I couldn't figure out the best way to end my life. The day I left the courtroom divorced and feeling desolate, believing my life was over. The day my daughters and I felt forced out of the home we loved. The day I wrote my first blog, feeling like I was starting life anew. To the day someone called needing encouraging words from little ole me. Each of these days lets me know that I was destined to be here and destined to be great!

Each and every one of us has a purpose. There's a reason why you showed up in this lifetime. It is up to you to figure out that purpose and hit the ground running. As long as you have breath in your body, it's never too late. Keep looking ahead. There's nothing behind you but the past, and your future is now! Make a vow today to live the rest of your life *naked*. Because this my friends, is the only way to live life authentically!

KEEP IT NAKED

A NOTE ON SOURCES

The author gratefully acknowledges the following works for their influence in writing this book: *The Holy Bible* and *The Seat of the Soul* by Gary Zukav.

ABOUT THE AUTHOR

Shemeka Michelle is an author, speaker and personal empowerment advocate. She's also a dedicated daughter, friend and mother of three.

Compiled life experiences led her to create Naked Girlz; a group of women who live transparent lives and speak about real topics. As a former ordained minister, Shemeka has over fifteen years of empowerment experience. Her honest and direct approach makes her advice simple and easy to follow.

Feeling empowered, she lives to inspire others to live life authentically. Willing to expose her deepest feelings in an effort to free not only herself, but facilitate the freedom of others, she lives by her mantra "Keep it NAKED!"

KEEPING UP WITH SHEMEKA MICHELLE....

You can keep up and stay abreast of all things

Shemeka Michelle at www.shemekamichelle.com.

In the meantime, thanks for reading the

book and don't forget to

Keep it NAKED!

Made in the USA
Las Vegas, NV
24 October 2021